SIMPLY
ORGANISED

NAME

EMAIL

Bibliografische Information der Deutschen Nationalbibliothek: Die
Deutsche Nationalbibliothek verzeichnet diese Publikation in der
Deutschen Nationalbibliografie; detaillierte bibliografische Daten
sind im Internet über dnb.dnb.de abrufbar.

© 2020 Lina Marie Walbracht
Herstellung und Verlag: BoD Books on Demand,
Norderstedt

ISBN: 978-375-267320-3

MADE WITH LOVE AND THOUGHTFULNESS

by LINA MARIE W.

MONDAY
28.12.2020

6	15
7	16
8	17
9	18
10	19
11	20
12	21
13	22
14	23

TUESDAY
29.12.2020

6	15
7	16
8	17
9	18
10	19
11	20
12	21
13	22
14	23

WEDNESDAY
30.12.2020

6	15
7	16
8	17
9	18
10	19
11	20
12	21
13	22
14	23

TO DO

- [ ] _____
- [ ] _____
- [ ] _____
- [ ] _____
- [ ] _____
- [ ] _____
- [ ] _____
- [ ] _____
- [ ] _____
- [ ] _____
- [ ] _____
- [ ] _____

- [ ] _____
- [ ] _____
- [ ] _____
- [ ] _____
- [ ] _____
- [ ] _____
- [ ] _____
- [ ] _____
- [ ] _____
- [ ] _____
- [ ] _____
- [ ] _____

NOTES

_____

_____

_____

_____

_____

_____

_____

_____

_____

_____

_____

_____

THURSDAY
31.12.2020

6	15
7	16
8	17
9	18
10	19
11	20
12	21
13	22
14	23

FRIDAY
01.01.2021

6	15
7	16
8	17
9	18
10	19
11	20
12	21
13	22
14	23

SATURDAY
02.01.2021

7
9
11
13
15
17
19
21
23

SUNDAY
03.01.2021

7
9
11
13
15
17
19
21
23

TO DO

- [ ] _____
- [ ] _____
- [ ] _____
- [ ] _____
- [ ] _____
- [ ] _____
- [ ] _____
- [ ] _____
- [ ] _____
- [ ] _____
- [ ] _____
- [ ] _____

- [ ] _____
- [ ] _____
- [ ] _____
- [ ] _____
- [ ] _____
- [ ] _____
- [ ] _____
- [ ] _____
- [ ] _____
- [ ] _____
- [ ] _____
- [ ] _____

NOTES

_____

_____

_____

_____

_____

_____

_____

_____

_____

_____

_____

_____

MONDAY
04.01.2021

6	15
7	16
8	17
9	18
10	19
11	20
12	21
13	22
14	23

TUESDAY
05.01.2021

6	15
7	16
8	17
9	18
10	19
11	20
12	21
13	22
14	23

WEDNESDAY
06.01.2021

6	15
7	16
8	17
9	18
10	19
11	20
12	21
13	22
14	23

TO DO

- [ ] _____
- [ ] _____
- [ ] _____
- [ ] _____
- [ ] _____
- [ ] _____
- [ ] _____
- [ ] _____
- [ ] _____
- [ ] _____
- [ ] _____
- [ ] _____

- [ ] _____
- [ ] _____
- [ ] _____
- [ ] _____
- [ ] _____
- [ ] _____
- [ ] _____
- [ ] _____
- [ ] _____
- [ ] _____
- [ ] _____
- [ ] _____

NOTES

_____
_____
_____
_____
_____
_____
_____
_____
_____
_____
_____
_____
_____
_____

THURSDAY
07.01.2021

6	15
7	16
8	17
9	18
10	19
11	20
12	21
13	22
14	23

FRIDAY
08.01.2021

6	15
7	16
8	17
9	18
10	19
11	20
12	21
13	22
14	23

SATURDAY
09.01.2021

7
9
11
13
15
17
19
21
23

SUNDAY
10.01.2021

7
9
11
13
15
17
19
21
23

TO DO

- [ ] _____
- [ ] _____
- [ ] _____
- [ ] _____
- [ ] _____
- [ ] _____
- [ ] _____
- [ ] _____
- [ ] _____
- [ ] _____
- [ ] _____
- [ ] _____

- [ ] _____
- [ ] _____
- [ ] _____
- [ ] _____
- [ ] _____
- [ ] _____
- [ ] _____
- [ ] _____
- [ ] _____
- [ ] _____
- [ ] _____
- [ ] _____

NOTES

_____

_____

_____

_____

_____

_____

_____

_____

_____

_____

_____

_____

_____

MONDAY
11.01.2021

6	15
7	16
8	17
9	18
10	19
11	20
12	21
13	22
14	23

TUESDAY
12.01.2021

6	15
7	16
8	17
9	18
10	19
11	20
12	21
13	22
14	23

WEDNESDAY
13.01.2021

6	15
7	16
8	17
9	18
10	19
11	20
12	21
13	22
14	23

TO DO

- [ ] _____
- [ ] _____
- [ ] _____
- [ ] _____
- [ ] _____
- [ ] _____
- [ ] _____
- [ ] _____
- [ ] _____
- [ ] _____
- [ ] _____
- [ ] _____

- [ ] _____
- [ ] _____
- [ ] _____
- [ ] _____
- [ ] _____
- [ ] _____
- [ ] _____
- [ ] _____
- [ ] _____
- [ ] _____
- [ ] _____
- [ ] _____

NOTES

_____

_____

_____

_____

_____

_____

_____

_____

_____

_____

_____

_____

_____

THURSDAY
14.01.2021

6	15
7	16
8	17
9	18
10	19
11	20
12	21
13	22
14	23

FRIDAY
15.01.2021

6	15
7	16
8	17
9	18
10	19
11	20
12	21
13	22
14	23

SATURDAY
16.01.2021

7
9
11
13
15
17
19
21
23

SUNDAY
17.01.2021

7
9
11
13
15
17
19
21
23

TO DO

- [ ] _____
- [ ] _____
- [ ] _____
- [ ] _____
- [ ] _____
- [ ] _____
- [ ] _____
- [ ] _____
- [ ] _____
- [ ] _____
- [ ] _____
- [ ] _____

- [ ] _____
- [ ] _____
- [ ] _____
- [ ] _____
- [ ] _____
- [ ] _____
- [ ] _____
- [ ] _____
- [ ] _____
- [ ] _____
- [ ] _____
- [ ] _____

NOTES

_____

_____

_____

_____

_____

_____

_____

_____

_____

_____

_____

_____

_____

MONDAY
18.01.2021

6	15
7	16
8	17
9	18
10	19
11	20
12	21
13	22
14	23

TUESDAY
19.01.2021

6	15
7	16
8	17
9	18
10	19
11	20
12	21
13	22
14	23

WEDNESDAY
20.01.2021

6	15
7	16
8	17
9	18
10	19
11	20
12	21
13	22
14	23

TO DO

- [ ] _____
- [ ] _____
- [ ] _____
- [ ] _____
- [ ] _____
- [ ] _____
- [ ] _____
- [ ] _____
- [ ] _____
- [ ] _____
- [ ] _____
- [ ] _____

- [ ] _____
- [ ] _____
- [ ] _____
- [ ] _____
- [ ] _____
- [ ] _____
- [ ] _____
- [ ] _____
- [ ] _____
- [ ] _____
- [ ] _____
- [ ] _____

NOTES

_____

_____

_____

_____

_____

_____

_____

_____

_____

_____

_____

_____

THURSDAY
21.01.2021

6	15
7	16
8	17
9	18
10	19
11	20
12	21
13	22
14	23

FRIDAY
22.01.2021

6	15
7	16
8	17
9	18
10	19
11	20
12	21
13	22
14	23

SATURDAY
23.01.2021

SUNDAY
24.01.2021

7	7
9	9
11	11
13	13
15	15
17	17
19	19
21	21
23	23

TO DO

- ☐ _____
- ☐ _____
- ☐ _____
- ☐ _____
- ☐ _____
- ☐ _____
- ☐ _____
- ☐ _____
- ☐ _____
- ☐ _____
- ☐ _____
- ☐ _____

- ☐ _____
- ☐ _____
- ☐ _____
- ☐ _____
- ☐ _____
- ☐ _____
- ☐ _____
- ☐ _____
- ☐ _____
- ☐ _____
- ☐ _____
- ☐ _____

NOTES

_____

_____

_____

_____

_____

_____

_____

_____

_____

_____

_____

_____

_____

MONDAY
25.01.2021

6	15
7	16
8	17
9	18
10	19
11	20
12	21
13	22
14	23

TUESDAY
26.01.2021

6	15
7	16
8	17
9	18
10	19
11	20
12	21
13	22
14	23

WEDNESDAY
27.01.2021

6	15
7	16
8	17
9	18
10	19
11	20
12	21
13	22
14	23

TO DO

- [ ] _____
- [ ] _____
- [ ] _____
- [ ] _____
- [ ] _____
- [ ] _____
- [ ] _____
- [ ] _____
- [ ] _____
- [ ] _____
- [ ] _____
- [ ] _____

- [ ] _____
- [ ] _____
- [ ] _____
- [ ] _____
- [ ] _____
- [ ] _____
- [ ] _____
- [ ] _____
- [ ] _____
- [ ] _____
- [ ] _____
- [ ] _____

NOTES

_____
_____
_____
_____
_____
_____
_____
_____
_____
_____
_____
_____
_____

THURSDAY
28.01.2021

6	15
7	16
8	17
9	18
10	19
11	20
12	21
13	22
14	23

FRIDAY
29.01.2021

6	15
7	16
8	17
9	18
10	19
11	20
12	21
13	22
14	23

SATURDAY
30.01.2021

7
9
11
13
15
17
19
21
23

SUNDAY
31.01.2021

7
9
11
13
15
17
19
21
23

TO DO

- [ ] _____
- [ ] _____
- [ ] _____
- [ ] _____
- [ ] _____
- [ ] _____
- [ ] _____
- [ ] _____
- [ ] _____
- [ ] _____
- [ ] _____
- [ ] _____

- [ ] _____
- [ ] _____
- [ ] _____
- [ ] _____
- [ ] _____
- [ ] _____
- [ ] _____
- [ ] _____
- [ ] _____
- [ ] _____
- [ ] _____
- [ ] _____

NOTES

_____

_____

_____

_____

_____

_____

_____

_____

_____

_____

_____

_____

_____

MONDAY
01.02.2021

6	15
7	16
8	17
9	18
10	19
11	20
12	21
13	22
14	23

TUESDAY
02.02.2021

6	15
7	16
8	17
9	18
10	19
11	20
12	21
13	22
14	23

WEDNESDAY
03.02.2021

6	15
7	16
8	17
9	18
10	19
11	20
12	21
13	22
14	23

TO DO

- [ ] _____
- [ ] _____
- [ ] _____
- [ ] _____
- [ ] _____
- [ ] _____
- [ ] _____
- [ ] _____
- [ ] _____
- [ ] _____
- [ ] _____
- [ ] _____

- [ ] _____
- [ ] _____
- [ ] _____
- [ ] _____
- [ ] _____
- [ ] _____
- [ ] _____
- [ ] _____
- [ ] _____
- [ ] _____
- [ ] _____
- [ ] _____

NOTES

_____

_____

_____

_____

_____

_____

_____

_____

_____

_____

_____

_____

THURSDAY
04.02.2021

6	15
7	16
8	17
9	18
10	19
11	20
12	21
13	22
14	23

FRIDAY
05.02.2021

6	15
7	16
8	17
9	18
10	19
11	20
12	21
13	22
14	23

SATURDAY
06.02.2021

7	
9	
11	
13	
15	
17	
19	
21	
23	

SUNDAY
07.02.2021

7	
9	
11	
13	
15	
17	
19	
21	
23	

TO DO

- [ ] _____
- [ ] _____
- [ ] _____
- [ ] _____
- [ ] _____
- [ ] _____
- [ ] _____
- [ ] _____
- [ ] _____
- [ ] _____
- [ ] _____
- [ ] _____

- [ ] _____
- [ ] _____
- [ ] _____
- [ ] _____
- [ ] _____
- [ ] _____
- [ ] _____
- [ ] _____
- [ ] _____
- [ ] _____
- [ ] _____
- [ ] _____

NOTES

_____

_____

_____

_____

_____

_____

_____

_____

_____

_____

_____

_____

_____

MONDAY
08.02.2021

6	15
7	16
8	17
9	18
10	19
11	20
12	21
13	22
14	23

TUESDAY
09.02.2021

6	15
7	16
8	17
9	18
10	19
11	20
12	21
13	22
14	23

WEDNESDAY
10.02.2021

6	15
7	16
8	17
9	18
10	19
11	20
12	21
13	22
14	23

TO DO

- [ ] _____
- [ ] _____
- [ ] _____
- [ ] _____
- [ ] _____
- [ ] _____
- [ ] _____
- [ ] _____
- [ ] _____
- [ ] _____
- [ ] _____
- [ ] _____

- [ ] _____
- [ ] _____
- [ ] _____
- [ ] _____
- [ ] _____
- [ ] _____
- [ ] _____
- [ ] _____
- [ ] _____
- [ ] _____
- [ ] _____
- [ ] _____

NOTES

_____

_____

_____

_____

_____

_____

_____

_____

_____

_____

_____

_____

THURSDAY
11.02.2021

6	15
7	16
8	17
9	18
10	19
11	20
12	21
13	22
14	23

FRIDAY
12.02.2021

6	15
7	16
8	17
9	18
10	19
11	20
12	21
13	22
14	23

SATURDAY
13.02.2021

7
9
11
13
15
17
19
21
23

SUNDAY
14.02.2021

7
9
11
13
15
17
19
21
23

TO DO

- [ ] _____
- [ ] _____
- [ ] _____
- [ ] _____
- [ ] _____
- [ ] _____
- [ ] _____
- [ ] _____
- [ ] _____
- [ ] _____
- [ ] _____
- [ ] _____

- [ ] _____
- [ ] _____
- [ ] _____
- [ ] _____
- [ ] _____
- [ ] _____
- [ ] _____
- [ ] _____
- [ ] _____
- [ ] _____
- [ ] _____
- [ ] _____

NOTES

_____

_____

_____

_____

_____

_____

_____

_____

_____

_____

_____

_____

MONDAY
15.02.2021

6		15	
7		16	
8		17	
9		18	
10		19	
11		20	
12		21	
13		22	
14		23	

TUESDAY
16.02.2021

6		15	
7		16	
8		17	
9		18	
10		19	
11		20	
12		21	
13		22	
14		23	

WEDNESDAY
17.02.2021

6		15	
7		16	
8		17	
9		18	
10		19	
11		20	
12		21	
13		22	
14		23	

TO DO

- [ ] _____
- [ ] _____
- [ ] _____
- [ ] _____
- [ ] _____
- [ ] _____
- [ ] _____
- [ ] _____
- [ ] _____
- [ ] _____
- [ ] _____
- [ ] _____

- [ ] _____
- [ ] _____
- [ ] _____
- [ ] _____
- [ ] _____
- [ ] _____
- [ ] _____
- [ ] _____
- [ ] _____
- [ ] _____
- [ ] _____
- [ ] _____

NOTES

_____

_____

_____

_____

_____

_____

_____

_____

_____

_____

_____

_____

THURSDAY
18.02.2021

6	15
7	16
8	17
9	18
10	19
11	20
12	21
13	22
14	23

FRIDAY
19.02.2021

6	15
7	16
8	17
9	18
10	19
11	20
12	21
13	22
14	23

SATURDAY
20.02.2021

7
9
11
13
15
17
19
21
23

SUNDAY
21.02.2021

7
9
11
13
15
17
19
21
23

TO DO

- [ ] _____
- [ ] _____
- [ ] _____
- [ ] _____
- [ ] _____
- [ ] _____
- [ ] _____
- [ ] _____
- [ ] _____
- [ ] _____
- [ ] _____
- [ ] _____

- [ ] _____
- [ ] _____
- [ ] _____
- [ ] _____
- [ ] _____
- [ ] _____
- [ ] _____
- [ ] _____
- [ ] _____
- [ ] _____
- [ ] _____
- [ ] _____

NOTES

_____

_____

_____

_____

_____

_____

_____

_____

_____

_____

_____

_____

_____

MONDAY
22.02.2021

6	15
7	16
8	17
9	18
10	19
11	20
12	21
13	22
14	23

TUESDAY
23.02.2021

6	15
7	16
8	17
9	18
10	19
11	20
12	21
13	22
14	23

WEDNESDAY
24.02.2021

6	15
7	16
8	17
9	18
10	19
11	20
12	21
13	22
14	23

TO DO

- [ ] _____
- [ ] _____
- [ ] _____
- [ ] _____
- [ ] _____
- [ ] _____
- [ ] _____
- [ ] _____
- [ ] _____
- [ ] _____
- [ ] _____
- [ ] _____

- [ ] _____
- [ ] _____
- [ ] _____
- [ ] _____
- [ ] _____
- [ ] _____
- [ ] _____
- [ ] _____
- [ ] _____
- [ ] _____
- [ ] _____
- [ ] _____

NOTES

_____

_____

_____

_____

_____

_____

_____

_____

_____

_____

_____

_____

_____

THURSDAY
25.02.2021

6	15
7	16
8	17
9	18
10	19
11	20
12	21
13	22
14	23

FRIDAY
26.02.2021

6	15
7	16
8	17
9	18
10	19
11	20
12	21
13	22
14	23

SATURDAY
27.02.2021

7
9
11
13
15
17
19
21
23

SUNDAY
28.02.2021

7
9
11
13
15
17
19
21
23

TO DO

☐ _____   ☐ _____
☐ _____   ☐ _____
☐ _____   ☐ _____
☐ _____   ☐ _____
☐ _____   ☐ _____
☐ _____   ☐ _____
☐ _____   ☐ _____
☐ _____   ☐ _____
☐ _____   ☐ _____
☐ _____   ☐ _____
☐ _____   ☐ _____
☐ _____   ☐ _____

NOTES

_____
_____
_____
_____
_____
_____
_____
_____
_____
_____
_____
_____
_____

MONDAY
01.03.2021

6	15
7	16
8	17
9	18
10	19
11	20
12	21
13	22
14	23

TUESDAY
02.03.2021

6	15
7	16
8	17
9	18
10	19
11	20
12	21
13	22
14	23

WEDNESDAY
03.03.2021

6	15
7	16
8	17
9	18
10	19
11	20
12	21
13	22
14	23

TO DO

☐ _____   ☐ _____
☐ _____   ☐ _____
☐ _____   ☐ _____
☐ _____   ☐ _____
☐ _____   ☐ _____
☐ _____   ☐ _____
☐ _____   ☐ _____
☐ _____   ☐ _____
☐ _____   ☐ _____
☐ _____   ☐ _____
☐ _____   ☐ _____
☐ _____   ☐ _____

NOTES

_____
_____
_____
_____
_____
_____
_____
_____
_____
_____
_____
_____
_____

THURSDAY
04.03.2021

6	15
7	16
8	17
9	18
10	19
11	20
12	21
13	22
14	23

FRIDAY
05.03.2021

6	15
7	16
8	17
9	18
10	19
11	20
12	21
13	22
14	23

SATURDAY
06.03.2021

7
9
11
13
15
17
19
21
23

SUNDAY
07.03.2021

7
9
11
13
15
17
19
21
23

TO DO

- [ ] _____
- [ ] _____
- [ ] _____
- [ ] _____
- [ ] _____
- [ ] _____
- [ ] _____
- [ ] _____
- [ ] _____
- [ ] _____
- [ ] _____
- [ ] _____

- [ ] _____
- [ ] _____
- [ ] _____
- [ ] _____
- [ ] _____
- [ ] _____
- [ ] _____
- [ ] _____
- [ ] _____
- [ ] _____
- [ ] _____
- [ ] _____

NOTES

_____

_____

_____

_____

_____

_____

_____

_____

_____

_____

_____

_____

MONDAY
08.03.2021

6	15
7	16
8	17
9	18
10	19
11	20
12	21
13	22
14	23

TUESDAY
09.03.2021

6	15
7	16
8	17
9	18
10	19
11	20
12	21
13	22
14	23

WEDNESDAY
10.03.2021

6	15
7	16
8	17
9	18
10	19
11	20
12	21
13	22
14	23

TO DO

- [ ] _____
- [ ] _____
- [ ] _____
- [ ] _____
- [ ] _____
- [ ] _____
- [ ] _____
- [ ] _____
- [ ] _____
- [ ] _____
- [ ] _____
- [ ] _____

- [ ] _____
- [ ] _____
- [ ] _____
- [ ] _____
- [ ] _____
- [ ] _____
- [ ] _____
- [ ] _____
- [ ] _____
- [ ] _____
- [ ] _____
- [ ] _____

NOTES

_____
_____
_____
_____
_____
_____
_____
_____
_____
_____
_____
_____
_____

THURSDAY
11.03.2021

6	15
7	16
8	17
9	18
10	19
11	20
12	21
13	22
14	23

FRIDAY
12.03.2021

6	15
7	16
8	17
9	18
10	19
11	20
12	21
13	22
14	23

SATURDAY
13.03.2021

7
9
11
13
15
17
19
21
23

SUNDAY
14.03.2021

7
9
11
13
15
17
19
21
23

TO DO

- [ ] _____
- [ ] _____
- [ ] _____
- [ ] _____
- [ ] _____
- [ ] _____
- [ ] _____
- [ ] _____
- [ ] _____
- [ ] _____
- [ ] _____
- [ ] _____

- [ ] _____
- [ ] _____
- [ ] _____
- [ ] _____
- [ ] _____
- [ ] _____
- [ ] _____
- [ ] _____
- [ ] _____
- [ ] _____
- [ ] _____
- [ ] _____

NOTES

_____

_____

_____

_____

_____

_____

_____

_____

_____

_____

_____

_____

_____

_____

MONDAY
15.03.2021

6	15
7	16
8	17
9	18
10	19
11	20
12	21
13	22
14	23

TUESDAY
16.03.2021

6	15
7	16
8	17
9	18
10	19
11	20
12	21
13	22
14	23

WEDNESDAY
17.03.2021

6	15
7	16
8	17
9	18
10	19
11	20
12	21
13	22
14	23

TO DO

- [ ] _____
- [ ] _____
- [ ] _____
- [ ] _____
- [ ] _____
- [ ] _____
- [ ] _____
- [ ] _____
- [ ] _____
- [ ] _____
- [ ] _____
- [ ] _____

- [ ] _____
- [ ] _____
- [ ] _____
- [ ] _____
- [ ] _____
- [ ] _____
- [ ] _____
- [ ] _____
- [ ] _____
- [ ] _____
- [ ] _____
- [ ] _____

NOTES

_____
_____
_____
_____
_____
_____
_____
_____
_____
_____
_____
_____
_____

THURSDAY
18.03.2021

6	15
7	16
8	17
9	18
10	19
11	20
12	21
13	22
14	23

FRIDAY
19.03.2021

6	15
7	16
8	17
9	18
10	19
11	20
12	21
13	22
14	23

SATURDAY
20.03.2021

7
9
11
13
15
17
19
21
23

SUNDAY
21.03.2021

7
9
11
13
15
17
19
21
23

TO DO

- [ ] _____
- [ ] _____
- [ ] _____
- [ ] _____
- [ ] _____
- [ ] _____
- [ ] _____
- [ ] _____
- [ ] _____
- [ ] _____
- [ ] _____
- [ ] _____

- [ ] _____
- [ ] _____
- [ ] _____
- [ ] _____
- [ ] _____
- [ ] _____
- [ ] _____
- [ ] _____
- [ ] _____
- [ ] _____
- [ ] _____
- [ ] _____

NOTES

_____

_____

_____

_____

_____

_____

_____

_____

_____

_____

_____

MONDAY
22.03.2021

6	15
7	16
8	17
9	18
10	19
11	20
12	21
13	22
14	23

TUESDAY
23.03.2021

6	15
7	16
8	17
9	18
10	19
11	20
12	21
13	22
14	23

WEDNESDAY
24.03.2021

6	15
7	16
8	17
9	18
10	19
11	20
12	21
13	22
14	23

TO DO

- [ ] _____
- [ ] _____
- [ ] _____
- [ ] _____
- [ ] _____
- [ ] _____
- [ ] _____
- [ ] _____
- [ ] _____
- [ ] _____
- [ ] _____
- [ ] _____

- [ ] _____
- [ ] _____
- [ ] _____
- [ ] _____
- [ ] _____
- [ ] _____
- [ ] _____
- [ ] _____
- [ ] _____
- [ ] _____
- [ ] _____
- [ ] _____

NOTES

_____

_____

_____

_____

_____

_____

_____

_____

_____

_____

_____

_____

THURSDAY
25.03.2021

6	15
7	16
8	17
9	18
10	19
11	20
12	21
13	22
14	23

FRIDAY
26.03.2021

6	15
7	16
8	17
9	18
10	19
11	20
12	21
13	22
14	23

SATURDAY
27.03.2021

7	
9	
11	
13	
15	
17	
19	
21	
23	

SUNDAY
28.03.2021

7	
9	
11	
13	
15	
17	
19	
21	
23	

TO DO

- ☐ _____
- ☐ _____
- ☐ _____
- ☐ _____
- ☐ _____
- ☐ _____
- ☐ _____
- ☐ _____
- ☐ _____
- ☐ _____
- ☐ _____
- ☐ _____

- ☐ _____
- ☐ _____
- ☐ _____
- ☐ _____
- ☐ _____
- ☐ _____
- ☐ _____
- ☐ _____
- ☐ _____
- ☐ _____
- ☐ _____
- ☐ _____

NOTES

_____

_____

_____

_____

_____

_____

_____

_____

_____

_____

_____

_____

MONDAY
29.03.2021

6	15
7	16
8	17
9	18
10	19
11	20
12	21
13	22
14	23

TUESDAY
30.03.2021

6	15
7	16
8	17
9	18
10	19
11	20
12	21
13	22
14	23

WEDNESDAY
31.03.2021

6	15
7	16
8	17
9	18
10	19
11	20
12	21
13	22
14	23

TO DO

- [ ] _____
- [ ] _____
- [ ] _____
- [ ] _____
- [ ] _____
- [ ] _____
- [ ] _____
- [ ] _____
- [ ] _____
- [ ] _____
- [ ] _____
- [ ] _____

- [ ] _____
- [ ] _____
- [ ] _____
- [ ] _____
- [ ] _____
- [ ] _____
- [ ] _____
- [ ] _____
- [ ] _____
- [ ] _____
- [ ] _____
- [ ] _____

NOTES

_____

_____

_____

_____

_____

_____

_____

_____

_____

_____

_____

_____

THURSDAY
01.04.2021

6	15
7	16
8	17
9	18
10	19
11	20
12	21
13	22
14	23

FRIDAY
02.04.2021

6	15
7	16
8	17
9	18
10	19
11	20
12	21
13	22
14	23

SATURDAY
03.04.2021

7
9
11
13
15
17
19
21
23

SUNDAY
04.04.2021

7
9
11
13
15
17
19
21
23

TO DO

- [ ] _____
- [ ] _____
- [ ] _____
- [ ] _____
- [ ] _____
- [ ] _____
- [ ] _____
- [ ] _____
- [ ] _____
- [ ] _____
- [ ] _____
- [ ] _____

- [ ] _____
- [ ] _____
- [ ] _____
- [ ] _____
- [ ] _____
- [ ] _____
- [ ] _____
- [ ] _____
- [ ] _____
- [ ] _____
- [ ] _____
- [ ] _____

NOTES

_____

_____

_____

_____

_____

_____

_____

_____

_____

_____

_____

_____

MONDAY
05.04.2021

6	15
7	16
8	17
9	18
10	19
11	20
12	21
13	22
14	23

TUESDAY
06.04.2021

6	15
7	16
8	17
9	18
10	19
11	20
12	21
13	22
14	23

WEDNESDAY
07.04.2021

6	15
7	16
8	17
9	18
10	19
11	20
12	21
13	22
14	23

TO DO

- [ ] _____
- [ ] _____
- [ ] _____
- [ ] _____
- [ ] _____
- [ ] _____
- [ ] _____
- [ ] _____
- [ ] _____
- [ ] _____
- [ ] _____
- [ ] _____

- [ ] _____
- [ ] _____
- [ ] _____
- [ ] _____
- [ ] _____
- [ ] _____
- [ ] _____
- [ ] _____
- [ ] _____
- [ ] _____
- [ ] _____
- [ ] _____

NOTES

_____

_____

_____

_____

_____

_____

_____

_____

_____

_____

_____

_____

THURSDAY
08.04.2021

6		15	
7		16	
8		17	
9		18	
10		19	
11		20	
12		21	
13		22	
14		23	

FRIDAY
09.04.2021

6		15	
7		16	
8		17	
9		18	
10		19	
11		20	
12		21	
13		22	
14		23	

SATURDAY
10.04.2021

7	
9	
11	
13	
15	
17	
19	
21	
23	

SUNDAY
11.04.2021

7	
9	
11	
13	
15	
17	
19	
21	
23	

TO DO

- [ ] _____
- [ ] _____
- [ ] _____
- [ ] _____
- [ ] _____
- [ ] _____
- [ ] _____
- [ ] _____
- [ ] _____
- [ ] _____
- [ ] _____
- [ ] _____

- [ ] _____
- [ ] _____
- [ ] _____
- [ ] _____
- [ ] _____
- [ ] _____
- [ ] _____
- [ ] _____
- [ ] _____
- [ ] _____
- [ ] _____
- [ ] _____

NOTES

_____

_____

_____

_____

_____

_____

_____

_____

_____

_____

_____

_____

_____

MONDAY
12.04.2021

6	15
7	16
8	17
9	18
10	19
11	20
12	21
13	22
14	23

TUESDAY
13.04.2021

6	15
7	16
8	17
9	18
10	19
11	20
12	21
13	22
14	23

WEDNESDAY
14.04.2021

6	15
7	16
8	17
9	18
10	19
11	20
12	21
13	22
14	23

TO DO

- [ ]
- [ ]
- [ ]
- [ ]
- [ ]
- [ ]
- [ ]
- [ ]
- [ ]
- [ ]
- [ ]
- [ ]

- [ ]
- [ ]
- [ ]
- [ ]
- [ ]
- [ ]
- [ ]
- [ ]
- [ ]
- [ ]
- [ ]
- [ ]

NOTES

THURSDAY
15.04.2021

6	15
7	16
8	17
9	18
10	19
11	20
12	21
13	22
14	23

FRIDAY
16.04.2021

6	15
7	16
8	17
9	18
10	19
11	20
12	21
13	22
14	23

SATURDAY
17.04.2021

7
9
11
13
15
17
19
21
23

SUNDAY
18.04.2021

7
9
11
13
15
17
19
21
23

TO DO

- [ ] _____
- [ ] _____
- [ ] _____
- [ ] _____
- [ ] _____
- [ ] _____
- [ ] _____
- [ ] _____
- [ ] _____
- [ ] _____
- [ ] _____
- [ ] _____

- [ ] _____
- [ ] _____
- [ ] _____
- [ ] _____
- [ ] _____
- [ ] _____
- [ ] _____
- [ ] _____
- [ ] _____
- [ ] _____
- [ ] _____
- [ ] _____

NOTES

_____
_____
_____
_____
_____
_____
_____
_____
_____
_____
_____
_____

MONDAY
19.04.2021

6	15
7	16
8	17
9	18
10	19
11	20
12	21
13	22
14	23

TUESDAY
20.04.2021

6	15
7	16
8	17
9	18
10	19
11	20
12	21
13	22
14	23

WEDNESDAY
21.04.2021

6	15
7	16
8	17
9	18
10	19
11	20
12	21
13	22
14	23

TO DO

☐ _____   ☐ _____
☐ _____   ☐ _____
☐ _____   ☐ _____
☐ _____   ☐ _____
☐ _____   ☐ _____
☐ _____   ☐ _____
☐ _____   ☐ _____
☐ _____   ☐ _____
☐ _____   ☐ _____
☐ _____   ☐ _____
☐ _____   ☐ _____
☐ _____   ☐ _____

NOTES

_____
_____
_____
_____
_____
_____
_____
_____
_____
_____
_____
_____

THURSDAY
22.04.2021

6	15
7	16
8	17
9	18
10	19
11	20
12	21
13	22
14	23

FRIDAY
23.04.2021

6	15
7	16
8	17
9	18
10	19
11	20
12	21
13	22
14	23

SATURDAY
24.04.2021

7	7
9	9
11	11
13	13
15	15
17	17
19	19
21	21
23	23

SUNDAY
25.04.2021

TO DO

- [ ]
- [ ]
- [ ]
- [ ]
- [ ]
- [ ]
- [ ]
- [ ]
- [ ]
- [ ]
- [ ]
- [ ]

- [ ]
- [ ]
- [ ]
- [ ]
- [ ]
- [ ]
- [ ]
- [ ]
- [ ]
- [ ]
- [ ]
- [ ]

NOTES

MONDAY
26.04.2021

6	15
7	16
8	17
9	18
10	19
11	20
12	21
13	22
14	23

TUESDAY
27.04.2021

6	15
7	16
8	17
9	18
10	19
11	20
12	21
13	22
14	23

WEDNESDAY
28.04.2021

6	15
7	16
8	17
9	18
10	19
11	20
12	21
13	22
14	23

TO DO

- [ ] _____
- [ ] _____
- [ ] _____
- [ ] _____
- [ ] _____
- [ ] _____
- [ ] _____
- [ ] _____
- [ ] _____
- [ ] _____
- [ ] _____
- [ ] _____

- [ ] _____
- [ ] _____
- [ ] _____
- [ ] _____
- [ ] _____
- [ ] _____
- [ ] _____
- [ ] _____
- [ ] _____
- [ ] _____
- [ ] _____
- [ ] _____

NOTES

_____

_____

_____

_____

_____

_____

_____

_____

_____

_____

_____

THURSDAY
29.04.2021

6	15
7	16
8	17
9	18
10	19
11	20
12	21
13	22
14	23

FRIDAY
30.04.2021

6	15
7	16
8	17
9	18
10	19
11	20
12	21
13	22
14	23

SATURDAY
01.05.2021

7
9
11
13
15
17
19
21
23

SUNDAY
02.05.2021

7
9
11
13
15
17
19
21
23

TO DO

☐ _____   ☐ _____
☐ _____   ☐ _____
☐ _____   ☐ _____
☐ _____   ☐ _____
☐ _____   ☐ _____
☐ _____   ☐ _____
☐ _____   ☐ _____
☐ _____   ☐ _____
☐ _____   ☐ _____
☐ _____   ☐ _____
☐ _____   ☐ _____
☐ _____   ☐ _____

NOTES

_____
_____
_____
_____
_____
_____
_____
_____
_____
_____
_____
_____

MONDAY
03.05.2021

6	15
7	16
8	17
9	18
10	19
11	20
12	21
13	22
14	23

TUESDAY
04.05.2021

6	15
7	16
8	17
9	18
10	19
11	20
12	21
13	22
14	23

WEDNESDAY
05.05.2021

6	15
7	16
8	17
9	18
10	19
11	20
12	21
13	22
14	23

TO DO

- [ ] _____
- [ ] _____
- [ ] _____
- [ ] _____
- [ ] _____
- [ ] _____
- [ ] _____
- [ ] _____
- [ ] _____
- [ ] _____
- [ ] _____
- [ ] _____

- [ ] _____
- [ ] _____
- [ ] _____
- [ ] _____
- [ ] _____
- [ ] _____
- [ ] _____
- [ ] _____
- [ ] _____
- [ ] _____
- [ ] _____
- [ ] _____

NOTES

_____

_____

_____

_____

_____

_____

_____

_____

_____

_____

_____

_____

_____

THURSDAY
06.05.2021

6	15
7	16
8	17
9	18
10	19
11	20
12	21
13	22
14	23

FRIDAY
07.05.2021

6	15
7	16
8	17
9	18
10	19
11	20
12	21
13	22
14	23

SATURDAY
08.05.2021

7
9
11
13
15
17
19
21
23

SUNDAY
09.05.2021

7
9
11
13
15
17
19
21
23

TO DO

- ☐ _____
- ☐ _____
- ☐ _____
- ☐ _____
- ☐ _____
- ☐ _____
- ☐ _____
- ☐ _____
- ☐ _____
- ☐ _____
- ☐ _____
- ☐ _____

- ☐ _____
- ☐ _____
- ☐ _____
- ☐ _____
- ☐ _____
- ☐ _____
- ☐ _____
- ☐ _____
- ☐ _____
- ☐ _____
- ☐ _____
- ☐ _____

NOTES

_____

_____

_____

_____

_____

_____

_____

_____

_____

_____

_____

_____

MONDAY
10.05.2021

6	15
7	16
8	17
9	18
10	19
11	20
12	21
13	22
14	23

TUESDAY
11.05.2021

6	15
7	16
8	17
9	18
10	19
11	20
12	21
13	22
14	23

WEDNESDAY
12.05.2021

6	15
7	16
8	17
9	18
10	19
11	20
12	21
13	22
14	23

TO DO

- [ ] _____
- [ ] _____
- [ ] _____
- [ ] _____
- [ ] _____
- [ ] _____
- [ ] _____
- [ ] _____
- [ ] _____
- [ ] _____
- [ ] _____
- [ ] _____

- [ ] _____
- [ ] _____
- [ ] _____
- [ ] _____
- [ ] _____
- [ ] _____
- [ ] _____
- [ ] _____
- [ ] _____
- [ ] _____
- [ ] _____
- [ ] _____

NOTES

_____
_____
_____
_____
_____
_____
_____
_____
_____
_____
_____
_____

THURSDAY
13.05.2021

6	15
7	16
8	17
9	18
10	19
11	20
12	21
13	22
14	23

FRIDAY
14.05.2021

6	15
7	16
8	17
9	18
10	19
11	20
12	21
13	22
14	23

SATURDAY
15.05.2021

7
9
11
13
15
17
19
21
23

SUNDAY
16.05.2021

7
9
11
13
15
17
19
21
23

TO DO

- [ ] _____
- [ ] _____
- [ ] _____
- [ ] _____
- [ ] _____
- [ ] _____
- [ ] _____
- [ ] _____
- [ ] _____
- [ ] _____
- [ ] _____
- [ ] _____

- [ ] _____
- [ ] _____
- [ ] _____
- [ ] _____
- [ ] _____
- [ ] _____
- [ ] _____
- [ ] _____
- [ ] _____
- [ ] _____
- [ ] _____
- [ ] _____

NOTES

MONDAY
17.05.2021

6	15
7	16
8	17
9	18
10	19
11	20
12	21
13	22
14	23

TUESDAY
18.05.2021

6	15
7	16
8	17
9	18
10	19
11	20
12	21
13	22
14	23

WEDNESDAY
19.05.2021

6	15
7	16
8	17
9	18
10	19
11	20
12	21
13	22
14	23

TO DO

- [ ] _____
- [ ] _____
- [ ] _____
- [ ] _____
- [ ] _____
- [ ] _____
- [ ] _____
- [ ] _____
- [ ] _____
- [ ] _____
- [ ] _____
- [ ] _____

- [ ] _____
- [ ] _____
- [ ] _____
- [ ] _____
- [ ] _____
- [ ] _____
- [ ] _____
- [ ] _____
- [ ] _____
- [ ] _____
- [ ] _____
- [ ] _____

NOTES

_____

_____

_____

_____

_____

_____

_____

_____

_____

_____

_____

_____

THURSDAY
20.05.2021

6	15
7	16
8	17
9	18
10	19
11	20
12	21
13	22
14	23

FRIDAY
21.05.2021

6	15
7	16
8	17
9	18
10	19
11	20
12	21
13	22
14	23

SATURDAY
22.05.2021

7	
9	
11	
13	
15	
17	
19	
21	
23	

SUNDAY
23.05.2021

7	
9	
11	
13	
15	
17	
19	
21	
23	

TO DO

☐ _____   ☐ _____
☐ _____   ☐ _____
☐ _____   ☐ _____
☐ _____   ☐ _____
☐ _____   ☐ _____
☐ _____   ☐ _____
☐ _____   ☐ _____
☐ _____   ☐ _____
☐ _____   ☐ _____
☐ _____   ☐ _____
☐ _____   ☐ _____
☐ _____   ☐ _____

NOTES

_____
_____
_____
_____
_____
_____
_____
_____
_____
_____
_____
_____
_____

MONDAY
24.05.2021

6	15
7	16
8	17
9	18
10	19
11	20
12	21
13	22
14	23

TUESDAY
25.05.2021

6	15
7	16
8	17
9	18
10	19
11	20
12	21
13	22
14	23

WEDNESDAY
26.05.2021

6	15
7	16
8	17
9	18
10	19
11	20
12	21
13	22
14	23

TO DO

- [ ] _____
- [ ] _____
- [ ] _____
- [ ] _____
- [ ] _____
- [ ] _____
- [ ] _____
- [ ] _____
- [ ] _____
- [ ] _____
- [ ] _____
- [ ] _____

- [ ] _____
- [ ] _____
- [ ] _____
- [ ] _____
- [ ] _____
- [ ] _____
- [ ] _____
- [ ] _____
- [ ] _____
- [ ] _____
- [ ] _____
- [ ] _____

NOTES

_____

_____

_____

_____

_____

_____

_____

_____

_____

_____

_____

_____

THURSDAY
27.05.2021

6	15
7	16
8	17
9	18
10	19
11	20
12	21
13	22
14	23

FRIDAY
28.05.2021

6	15
7	16
8	17
9	18
10	19
11	20
12	21
13	22
14	23

SATURDAY
29.05.2021

7	7
9	9
11	11
13	13
15	15
17	17
19	19
21	21
23	23

SUNDAY
30.05.2021

TO DO

- [ ] _____
- [ ] _____
- [ ] _____
- [ ] _____
- [ ] _____
- [ ] _____
- [ ] _____
- [ ] _____
- [ ] _____
- [ ] _____
- [ ] _____
- [ ] _____

- [ ] _____
- [ ] _____
- [ ] _____
- [ ] _____
- [ ] _____
- [ ] _____
- [ ] _____
- [ ] _____
- [ ] _____
- [ ] _____
- [ ] _____
- [ ] _____

NOTES

_____

_____

_____

_____

_____

_____

_____

_____

_____

_____

_____

_____

MONDAY
31.05.2021

6	15
7	16
8	17
9	18
10	19
11	20
12	21
13	22
14	23

TUESDAY
01.06.2021

6	15
7	16
8	17
9	18
10	19
11	20
12	21
13	22
14	23

WEDNESDAY
02.06.2021

6	15
7	16
8	17
9	18
10	19
11	20
12	21
13	22
14	23

TO DO

- ☐ _____
- ☐ _____
- ☐ _____
- ☐ _____
- ☐ _____
- ☐ _____
- ☐ _____
- ☐ _____
- ☐ _____
- ☐ _____
- ☐ _____
- ☐ _____

- ☐ _____
- ☐ _____
- ☐ _____
- ☐ _____
- ☐ _____
- ☐ _____
- ☐ _____
- ☐ _____
- ☐ _____
- ☐ _____
- ☐ _____
- ☐ _____

NOTES

_____

_____

_____

_____

_____

_____

_____

_____

_____

_____

_____

_____

THURSDAY
03.06.2021

6	15
7	16
8	17
9	18
10	19
11	20
12	21
13	22
14	23

FRIDAY
04.06.2021

6	15
7	16
8	17
9	18
10	19
11	20
12	21
13	22
14	23

SATURDAY
05.06.2021

7
9
11
13
15
17
19
21
23

SUNDAY
06.06.2021

7
9
11
13
15
17
19
21
23

TO DO

- [ ] _____
- [ ] _____
- [ ] _____
- [ ] _____
- [ ] _____
- [ ] _____
- [ ] _____
- [ ] _____
- [ ] _____
- [ ] _____
- [ ] _____
- [ ] _____

- [ ] _____
- [ ] _____
- [ ] _____
- [ ] _____
- [ ] _____
- [ ] _____
- [ ] _____
- [ ] _____
- [ ] _____
- [ ] _____
- [ ] _____
- [ ] _____

NOTES

MONDAY
07.06.2021

6	15
7	16
8	17
9	18
10	19
11	20
12	21
13	22
14	23

TUESDAY
08.06.2021

6	15
7	16
8	17
9	18
10	19
11	20
12	21
13	22
14	23

WEDNESDAY
09.06.2021

6	15
7	16
8	17
9	18
10	19
11	20
12	21
13	22
14	23

TO DO

- [ ] _____
- [ ] _____
- [ ] _____
- [ ] _____
- [ ] _____
- [ ] _____
- [ ] _____
- [ ] _____
- [ ] _____
- [ ] _____
- [ ] _____
- [ ] _____

- [ ] _____
- [ ] _____
- [ ] _____
- [ ] _____
- [ ] _____
- [ ] _____
- [ ] _____
- [ ] _____
- [ ] _____
- [ ] _____
- [ ] _____
- [ ] _____

NOTES

_____

_____

_____

_____

_____

_____

_____

_____

_____

_____

_____

_____

THURSDAY
10.06.2021

6	15
7	16
8	17
9	18
10	19
11	20
12	21
13	22
14	23

FRIDAY
11.06.2021

6	15
7	16
8	17
9	18
10	19
11	20
12	21
13	22
14	23

SATURDAY
12.06.2021

7
9
11
13
15
17
19
21
23

SUNDAY
13.06.2021

7
9
11
13
15
17
19
21
23

TO DO

- [ ] _____
- [ ] _____
- [ ] _____
- [ ] _____
- [ ] _____
- [ ] _____
- [ ] _____
- [ ] _____
- [ ] _____
- [ ] _____
- [ ] _____
- [ ] _____

- [ ] _____
- [ ] _____
- [ ] _____
- [ ] _____
- [ ] _____
- [ ] _____
- [ ] _____
- [ ] _____
- [ ] _____
- [ ] _____
- [ ] _____
- [ ] _____

NOTES

MONDAY
14.06.2021

6	15
7	16
8	17
9	18
10	19
11	20
12	21
13	22
14	23

TUESDAY
15.06.2021

6	15
7	16
8	17
9	18
10	19
11	20
12	21
13	22
14	23

WEDNESDAY
16.06.2021

6	15
7	16
8	17
9	18
10	19
11	20
12	21
13	22
14	23

TO DO

- [ ] _____
- [ ] _____
- [ ] _____
- [ ] _____
- [ ] _____
- [ ] _____
- [ ] _____
- [ ] _____
- [ ] _____
- [ ] _____
- [ ] _____
- [ ] _____

- [ ] _____
- [ ] _____
- [ ] _____
- [ ] _____
- [ ] _____
- [ ] _____
- [ ] _____
- [ ] _____
- [ ] _____
- [ ] _____
- [ ] _____
- [ ] _____

NOTES

THURSDAY
17.06.2021

6	15
7	16
8	17
9	18
10	19
11	20
12	21
13	22
14	23

FRIDAY
18.06.2021

6	15
7	16
8	17
9	18
10	19
11	20
12	21
13	22
14	23

SATURDAY
19.06.2021

SUNDAY
20.06.2021

7	7
9	9
11	11
13	13
15	15
17	17
19	19
21	21
23	23

TO DO

- [ ] _____
- [ ] _____
- [ ] _____
- [ ] _____
- [ ] _____
- [ ] _____
- [ ] _____
- [ ] _____
- [ ] _____
- [ ] _____
- [ ] _____
- [ ] _____

- [ ] _____
- [ ] _____
- [ ] _____
- [ ] _____
- [ ] _____
- [ ] _____
- [ ] _____
- [ ] _____
- [ ] _____
- [ ] _____
- [ ] _____
- [ ] _____

NOTES

_____

_____

_____

_____

_____

_____

_____

_____

_____

_____

_____

_____

_____

MONDAY
21.06.2021

6	15
7	16
8	17
9	18
10	19
11	20
12	21
13	22
14	23

TUESDAY
22.06.2021

6	15
7	16
8	17
9	18
10	19
11	20
12	21
13	22
14	23

WEDNESDAY
23.06.2021

6	15
7	16
8	17
9	18
10	19
11	20
12	21
13	22
14	23

TO DO

- [ ] _____
- [ ] _____
- [ ] _____
- [ ] _____
- [ ] _____
- [ ] _____
- [ ] _____
- [ ] _____
- [ ] _____
- [ ] _____
- [ ] _____
- [ ] _____

- [ ] _____
- [ ] _____
- [ ] _____
- [ ] _____
- [ ] _____
- [ ] _____
- [ ] _____
- [ ] _____
- [ ] _____
- [ ] _____
- [ ] _____
- [ ] _____

NOTES

_____

_____

_____

_____

_____

_____

_____

_____

_____

_____

_____

_____

_____

THURSDAY
24.06.2021

6	15
7	16
8	17
9	18
10	19
11	20
12	21
13	22
14	23

FRIDAY
25.06.2021

6	15
7	16
8	17
9	18
10	19
11	20
12	21
13	22
14	23

SATURDAY
26.06.2021

7	7
9	9
11	11
13	13
15	15
17	17
19	19
21	21
23	23

SUNDAY
27.06.2021

TO DO

- [ ]
- [ ]
- [ ]
- [ ]
- [ ]
- [ ]
- [ ]
- [ ]
- [ ]
- [ ]
- [ ]
- [ ]

- [ ]
- [ ]
- [ ]
- [ ]
- [ ]
- [ ]
- [ ]
- [ ]
- [ ]
- [ ]
- [ ]
- [ ]

NOTES

MONDAY
28.06.2021

6	15
7	16
8	17
9	18
10	19
11	20
12	21
13	22
14	23

TUESDAY
29.06.2021

6	15
7	16
8	17
9	18
10	19
11	20
12	21
13	22
14	23

WEDNESDAY
30.06.2021

6	15
7	16
8	17
9	18
10	19
11	20
12	21
13	22
14	23

TO DO

- [ ] _____
- [ ] _____
- [ ] _____
- [ ] _____
- [ ] _____
- [ ] _____
- [ ] _____
- [ ] _____
- [ ] _____
- [ ] _____
- [ ] _____
- [ ] _____

- [ ] _____
- [ ] _____
- [ ] _____
- [ ] _____
- [ ] _____
- [ ] _____
- [ ] _____
- [ ] _____
- [ ] _____
- [ ] _____
- [ ] _____
- [ ] _____

NOTES

_____

_____

_____

_____

_____

_____

_____

_____

_____

_____

_____

THURSDAY
01.07.2021

6	15
7	16
8	17
9	18
10	19
11	20
12	21
13	22
14	23

FRIDAY
02.07.2021

6	15
7	16
8	17
9	18
10	19
11	20
12	21
13	22
14	23

SATURDAY
03.07.2021

7
9
11
13
15
17
19
21
23

SUNDAY
04.07.2021

7
9
11
13
15
17
19
21
23

TO DO

☐ _____   ☐ _____
☐ _____   ☐ _____
☐ _____   ☐ _____
☐ _____   ☐ _____
☐ _____   ☐ _____
☐ _____   ☐ _____
☐ _____   ☐ _____
☐ _____   ☐ _____
☐ _____   ☐ _____
☐ _____   ☐ _____
☐ _____   ☐ _____
☐ _____   ☐ _____

NOTES

_____
_____
_____
_____
_____
_____
_____
_____
_____
_____
_____
_____
_____

MONDAY
05.07.2021

6	15
7	16
8	17
9	18
10	19
11	20
12	21
13	22
14	23

TUESDAY
06.07.2021

6	15
7	16
8	17
9	18
10	19
11	20
12	21
13	22
14	23

WEDNESDAY
07.07.2021

6	15
7	16
8	17
9	18
10	19
11	20
12	21
13	22
14	23

TO DO

- [ ] _____
- [ ] _____
- [ ] _____
- [ ] _____
- [ ] _____
- [ ] _____
- [ ] _____
- [ ] _____
- [ ] _____
- [ ] _____
- [ ] _____
- [ ] _____

- [ ] _____
- [ ] _____
- [ ] _____
- [ ] _____
- [ ] _____
- [ ] _____
- [ ] _____
- [ ] _____
- [ ] _____
- [ ] _____
- [ ] _____
- [ ] _____

NOTES

THURSDAY
08.07.2021

6	15
7	16
8	17
9	18
10	19
11	20
12	21
13	22
14	23

FRIDAY
09.07.2021

6	15
7	16
8	17
9	18
10	19
11	20
12	21
13	22
14	23

SATURDAY
10.07.2021

7
9
11
13
15
17
19
21
23

SUNDAY
11.07.2021

7
9
11
13
15
17
19
21
23

TO DO

- [ ]
- [ ]
- [ ]
- [ ]
- [ ]
- [ ]
- [ ]
- [ ]
- [ ]
- [ ]
- [ ]
- [ ]

- [ ]
- [ ]
- [ ]
- [ ]
- [ ]
- [ ]
- [ ]
- [ ]
- [ ]
- [ ]
- [ ]
- [ ]

NOTES

MONDAY
12.07.2021

6	15
7	16
8	17
9	18
10	19
11	20
12	21
13	22
14	23

TUESDAY
13.07.2021

6	15
7	16
8	17
9	18
10	19
11	20
12	21
13	22
14	23

WEDNESDAY
14.07.2021

6	15
7	16
8	17
9	18
10	19
11	20
12	21
13	22
14	23

TO DO

- [ ] _____
- [ ] _____
- [ ] _____
- [ ] _____
- [ ] _____
- [ ] _____
- [ ] _____
- [ ] _____
- [ ] _____
- [ ] _____
- [ ] _____
- [ ] _____

- [ ] _____
- [ ] _____
- [ ] _____
- [ ] _____
- [ ] _____
- [ ] _____
- [ ] _____
- [ ] _____
- [ ] _____
- [ ] _____
- [ ] _____
- [ ] _____

NOTES

_____

_____

_____

_____

_____

_____

_____

_____

_____

_____

_____

_____

THURSDAY
15.07.2021

6	15
7	16
8	17
9	18
10	19
11	20
12	21
13	22
14	23

FRIDAY
16.07.2021

6	15
7	16
8	17
9	18
10	19
11	20
12	21
13	22
14	23

SATURDAY
17.07.2021

7	
9	
11	
13	
15	
17	
19	
21	
23	

SUNDAY
18.07.2021

7	
9	
11	
13	
15	
17	
19	
21	
23	

TO DO

- [ ]
- [ ]
- [ ]
- [ ]
- [ ]
- [ ]
- [ ]
- [ ]
- [ ]
- [ ]
- [ ]
- [ ]

- [ ]
- [ ]
- [ ]
- [ ]
- [ ]
- [ ]
- [ ]
- [ ]
- [ ]
- [ ]
- [ ]
- [ ]

NOTES

MONDAY
19.07.2021

6	15
7	16
8	17
9	18
10	19
11	20
12	21
13	22
14	23

TUESDAY
20.07.2021

6	15
7	16
8	17
9	18
10	19
11	20
12	21
13	22
14	23

WEDNESDAY
21.07.2021

6	15
7	16
8	17
9	18
10	19
11	20
12	21
13	22
14	23

TO DO

- [ ] _____
- [ ] _____
- [ ] _____
- [ ] _____
- [ ] _____
- [ ] _____
- [ ] _____
- [ ] _____
- [ ] _____
- [ ] _____
- [ ] _____
- [ ] _____

- [ ] _____
- [ ] _____
- [ ] _____
- [ ] _____
- [ ] _____
- [ ] _____
- [ ] _____
- [ ] _____
- [ ] _____
- [ ] _____
- [ ] _____
- [ ] _____

NOTES

_____

_____

_____

_____

_____

_____

_____

_____

_____

_____

_____

_____

THURSDAY
22.07.2021

6	15
7	16
8	17
9	18
10	19
11	20
12	21
13	22
14	23

FRIDAY
23.07.2021

6	15
7	16
8	17
9	18
10	19
11	20
12	21
13	22
14	23

SATURDAY
24.07.2021

7
9
11
13
15
17
19
21
23

SUNDAY
25.07.2021

7
9
11
13
15
17
19
21
23

TO DO

- [ ] _____
- [ ] _____
- [ ] _____
- [ ] _____
- [ ] _____
- [ ] _____
- [ ] _____
- [ ] _____
- [ ] _____
- [ ] _____
- [ ] _____
- [ ] _____

- [ ] _____
- [ ] _____
- [ ] _____
- [ ] _____
- [ ] _____
- [ ] _____
- [ ] _____
- [ ] _____
- [ ] _____
- [ ] _____
- [ ] _____
- [ ] _____

NOTES

_____

_____

_____

_____

_____

_____

_____

_____

_____

_____

_____

_____

MONDAY
26.07.2021

6	15
7	16
8	17
9	18
10	19
11	20
12	21
13	22
14	23

TUESDAY
27.07.2021

6	15
7	16
8	17
9	18
10	19
11	20
12	21
13	22
14	23

WEDNESDAY
28.07.2021

6	15
7	16
8	17
9	18
10	19
11	20
12	21
13	22
14	23

TO DO

- [ ] _____
- [ ] _____
- [ ] _____
- [ ] _____
- [ ] _____
- [ ] _____
- [ ] _____
- [ ] _____
- [ ] _____
- [ ] _____
- [ ] _____
- [ ] _____

- [ ] _____
- [ ] _____
- [ ] _____
- [ ] _____
- [ ] _____
- [ ] _____
- [ ] _____
- [ ] _____
- [ ] _____
- [ ] _____
- [ ] _____
- [ ] _____

NOTES

THURSDAY
29.07.2021

6	15
7	16
8	17
9	18
10	19
11	20
12	21
13	22
14	23

FRIDAY
30.07.2021

6	15
7	16
8	17
9	18
10	19
11	20
12	21
13	22
14	23

SATURDAY
31.07.2021

SUNDAY
01.08.2021

SATURDAY	SUNDAY
7	7
9	9
11	11
13	13
15	15
17	17
19	19
21	21
23	23

TO DO

- [ ] _____
- [ ] _____
- [ ] _____
- [ ] _____
- [ ] _____
- [ ] _____
- [ ] _____
- [ ] _____
- [ ] _____
- [ ] _____
- [ ] _____
- [ ] _____

- [ ] _____
- [ ] _____
- [ ] _____
- [ ] _____
- [ ] _____
- [ ] _____
- [ ] _____
- [ ] _____
- [ ] _____
- [ ] _____
- [ ] _____
- [ ] _____

NOTES

MONDAY
02.08.2021

6	15
7	16
8	17
9	18
10	19
11	20
12	21
13	22
14	23

TUESDAY
03.08.2021

6	15
7	16
8	17
9	18
10	19
11	20
12	21
13	22
14	23

WEDNESDAY
04.08.2021

6	15
7	16
8	17
9	18
10	19
11	20
12	21
13	22
14	23

TO DO

- [ ] _____
- [ ] _____
- [ ] _____
- [ ] _____
- [ ] _____
- [ ] _____
- [ ] _____
- [ ] _____
- [ ] _____
- [ ] _____
- [ ] _____
- [ ] _____

- [ ] _____
- [ ] _____
- [ ] _____
- [ ] _____
- [ ] _____
- [ ] _____
- [ ] _____
- [ ] _____
- [ ] _____
- [ ] _____
- [ ] _____
- [ ] _____

NOTES

_____

_____

_____

_____

_____

_____

_____

_____

_____

_____

_____

_____

THURSDAY
05.08.2021

6	15
7	16
8	17
9	18
10	19
11	20
12	21
13	22
14	23

FRIDAY
06.08.2021

6	15
7	16
8	17
9	18
10	19
11	20
12	21
13	22
14	23

SATURDAY
07.08.2021

7	7
9	9
11	11
13	13
15	15
17	17
19	19
21	21
23	23

SUNDAY
08.08.2021

TO DO

- [ ]
- [ ]
- [ ]
- [ ]
- [ ]
- [ ]
- [ ]
- [ ]
- [ ]
- [ ]
- [ ]
- [ ]

- [ ]
- [ ]
- [ ]
- [ ]
- [ ]
- [ ]
- [ ]
- [ ]
- [ ]
- [ ]
- [ ]
- [ ]

NOTES

MONDAY
09.08.2021

6	15
7	16
8	17
9	18
10	19
11	20
12	21
13	22
14	23

TUESDAY
10.08.2021

6	15
7	16
8	17
9	18
10	19
11	20
12	21
13	22
14	23

WEDNESDAY
11.08.2021

6	15
7	16
8	17
9	18
10	19
11	20
12	21
13	22
14	23

TO DO

☐ _____   ☐ _____
☐ _____   ☐ _____
☐ _____   ☐ _____
☐ _____   ☐ _____
☐ _____   ☐ _____
☐ _____   ☐ _____
☐ _____   ☐ _____
☐ _____   ☐ _____
☐ _____   ☐ _____
☐ _____   ☐ _____
☐ _____   ☐ _____
☐ _____   ☐ _____

NOTES

_____
_____
_____
_____
_____
_____
_____
_____
_____
_____
_____
_____

THURSDAY
12.08.2021

6		15	
7		16	
8		17	
9		18	
10		19	
11		20	
12		21	
13		22	
14		23	

FRIDAY
13.08.2021

6		15	
7		16	
8		17	
9		18	
10		19	
11		20	
12		21	
13		22	
14		23	

SATURDAY
14.08.2021

	SUNDAY	
7	7	
9	9	
11	11	
13	13	
15	15	
17	17	
19	19	
21	21	
23	23	

SUNDAY
15.08.2021

TO DO

- ☐ _____
- ☐ _____
- ☐ _____
- ☐ _____
- ☐ _____
- ☐ _____
- ☐ _____
- ☐ _____
- ☐ _____
- ☐ _____
- ☐ _____
- ☐ _____

- ☐ _____
- ☐ _____
- ☐ _____
- ☐ _____
- ☐ _____
- ☐ _____
- ☐ _____
- ☐ _____
- ☐ _____
- ☐ _____
- ☐ _____
- ☐ _____

NOTES

_____

_____

_____

_____

_____

_____

_____

_____

_____

_____

_____

_____

MONDAY
16.08.2021

6	15
7	16
8	17
9	18
10	19
11	20
12	21
13	22
14	23

TUESDAY
17.08.2021

6	15
7	16
8	17
9	18
10	19
11	20
12	21
13	22
14	23

WEDNESDAY
18.08.2021

6	15
7	16
8	17
9	18
10	19
11	20
12	21
13	22
14	23

TO DO

- [ ] _____
- [ ] _____
- [ ] _____
- [ ] _____
- [ ] _____
- [ ] _____
- [ ] _____
- [ ] _____
- [ ] _____
- [ ] _____
- [ ] _____
- [ ] _____

- [ ] _____
- [ ] _____
- [ ] _____
- [ ] _____
- [ ] _____
- [ ] _____
- [ ] _____
- [ ] _____
- [ ] _____
- [ ] _____
- [ ] _____
- [ ] _____

NOTES

_____

_____

_____

_____

_____

_____

_____

_____

_____

_____

_____

_____

THURSDAY
19.08.2021

6	15
7	16
8	17
9	18
10	19
11	20
12	21
13	22
14	23

FRIDAY
20.08.2021

6	15
7	16
8	17
9	18
10	19
11	20
12	21
13	22
14	23

SATURDAY
21.08.2021

7
9
11
13
15
17
19
21
23

SUNDAY
22.08.2021

7
9
11
13
15
17
19
21
23

TO DO

- [ ] _____
- [ ] _____
- [ ] _____
- [ ] _____
- [ ] _____
- [ ] _____
- [ ] _____
- [ ] _____
- [ ] _____
- [ ] _____
- [ ] _____
- [ ] _____

- [ ] _____
- [ ] _____
- [ ] _____
- [ ] _____
- [ ] _____
- [ ] _____
- [ ] _____
- [ ] _____
- [ ] _____
- [ ] _____
- [ ] _____
- [ ] _____

NOTES

_____

_____

_____

_____

_____

_____

_____

_____

_____

_____

_____

_____

_____

MONDAY
23.08.2021

6	15
7	16
8	17
9	18
10	19
11	20
12	21
13	22
14	23

TUESDAY
24.08.2021

6	15
7	16
8	17
9	18
10	19
11	20
12	21
13	22
14	23

WEDNESDAY
25.08.2021

6	15
7	16
8	17
9	18
10	19
11	20
12	21
13	22
14	23

TO DO

- [ ] _____
- [ ] _____
- [ ] _____
- [ ] _____
- [ ] _____
- [ ] _____
- [ ] _____
- [ ] _____
- [ ] _____
- [ ] _____
- [ ] _____
- [ ] _____

- [ ] _____
- [ ] _____
- [ ] _____
- [ ] _____
- [ ] _____
- [ ] _____
- [ ] _____
- [ ] _____
- [ ] _____
- [ ] _____
- [ ] _____
- [ ] _____

NOTES

_____
_____
_____
_____
_____
_____
_____
_____
_____
_____
_____
_____
_____

THURSDAY
26.08.2021

6	15
7	16
8	17
9	18
10	19
11	20
12	21
13	22
14	23

FRIDAY
27.08.2021

6	15
7	16
8	17
9	18
10	19
11	20
12	21
13	22
14	23

SATURDAY
28.08.2021

7	
9	
11	
13	
15	
17	
19	
21	
23	

SUNDAY
29.08.2021

7	
9	
11	
13	
15	
17	
19	
21	
23	

TO DO

- [ ]
- [ ]
- [ ]
- [ ]
- [ ]
- [ ]
- [ ]
- [ ]
- [ ]
- [ ]
- [ ]
- [ ]

- [ ]
- [ ]
- [ ]
- [ ]
- [ ]
- [ ]
- [ ]
- [ ]
- [ ]
- [ ]
- [ ]
- [ ]

NOTES

MONDAY
30.08.2021

6	15
7	16
8	17
9	18
10	19
11	20
12	21
13	22
14	23

TUESDAY
31.08.2021

6	15
7	16
8	17
9	18
10	19
11	20
12	21
13	22
14	23

WEDNESDAY
01.09.2021

6	15
7	16
8	17
9	18
10	19
11	20
12	21
13	22
14	23

TO DO

- [ ] _____
- [ ] _____
- [ ] _____
- [ ] _____
- [ ] _____
- [ ] _____
- [ ] _____
- [ ] _____
- [ ] _____
- [ ] _____
- [ ] _____
- [ ] _____

- [ ] _____
- [ ] _____
- [ ] _____
- [ ] _____
- [ ] _____
- [ ] _____
- [ ] _____
- [ ] _____
- [ ] _____
- [ ] _____
- [ ] _____
- [ ] _____

NOTES

THURSDAY
02.09.2021

6	15
7	16
8	17
9	18
10	19
11	20
12	21
13	22
14	23

FRIDAY
03.09.2021

6	15
7	16
8	17
9	18
10	19
11	20
12	21
13	22
14	23

SATURDAY
04.09.2021

7
9
11
13
15
17
19
21
23

SUNDAY
05.09.2021

7
9
11
13
15
17
19
21
23

TO DO

- [ ] _____
- [ ] _____
- [ ] _____
- [ ] _____
- [ ] _____
- [ ] _____
- [ ] _____
- [ ] _____
- [ ] _____
- [ ] _____
- [ ] _____
- [ ] _____

- [ ] _____
- [ ] _____
- [ ] _____
- [ ] _____
- [ ] _____
- [ ] _____
- [ ] _____
- [ ] _____
- [ ] _____
- [ ] _____
- [ ] _____
- [ ] _____

NOTES

_____

_____

_____

_____

_____

_____

_____

_____

_____

_____

_____

_____

_____

MONDAY
06.09.2021

6	15
7	16
8	17
9	18
10	19
11	20
12	21
13	22
14	23

TUESDAY
07.09.2021

6	15
7	16
8	17
9	18
10	19
11	20
12	21
13	22
14	23

WEDNESDAY
08.09.2021

6	15
7	16
8	17
9	18
10	19
11	20
12	21
13	22
14	23

TO DO

- [ ] _____
- [ ] _____
- [ ] _____
- [ ] _____
- [ ] _____
- [ ] _____
- [ ] _____
- [ ] _____
- [ ] _____
- [ ] _____
- [ ] _____
- [ ] _____

- [ ] _____
- [ ] _____
- [ ] _____
- [ ] _____
- [ ] _____
- [ ] _____
- [ ] _____
- [ ] _____
- [ ] _____
- [ ] _____
- [ ] _____
- [ ] _____

NOTES

_____

_____

_____

_____

_____

_____

_____

_____

_____

_____

_____

_____

THURSDAY
09.09.2021

6	15
7	16
8	17
9	18
10	19
11	20
12	21
13	22
14	23

FRIDAY
10.09.2021

6	15
7	16
8	17
9	18
10	19
11	20
12	21
13	22
14	23

SATURDAY
11.09.2021

7
9
11
13
15
17
19
21
23

SUNDAY
12.09.2021

7
9
11
13
15
17
19
21
23

TO DO

- [ ] _____
- [ ] _____
- [ ] _____
- [ ] _____
- [ ] _____
- [ ] _____
- [ ] _____
- [ ] _____
- [ ] _____
- [ ] _____
- [ ] _____
- [ ] _____

- [ ] _____
- [ ] _____
- [ ] _____
- [ ] _____
- [ ] _____
- [ ] _____
- [ ] _____
- [ ] _____
- [ ] _____
- [ ] _____
- [ ] _____
- [ ] _____

NOTES

_____

_____

_____

_____

_____

_____

_____

_____

_____

_____

_____

_____

_____

MONDAY
13.09.2021

6	15
7	16
8	17
9	18
10	19
11	20
12	21
13	22
14	23

TUESDAY
14.09.2021

6	15
7	16
8	17
9	18
10	19
11	20
12	21
13	22
14	23

WEDNESDAY
15.09.2021

6	15
7	16
8	17
9	18
10	19
11	20
12	21
13	22
14	23

TO DO

- [ ]
- [ ]
- [ ]
- [ ]
- [ ]
- [ ]
- [ ]
- [ ]
- [ ]
- [ ]
- [ ]
- [ ]

- [ ]
- [ ]
- [ ]
- [ ]
- [ ]
- [ ]
- [ ]
- [ ]
- [ ]
- [ ]
- [ ]
- [ ]

NOTES

THURSDAY
16.09.2021

6	15
7	16
8	17
9	18
10	19
11	20
12	21
13	22
14	23

FRIDAY
17.09.2021

6	15
7	16
8	17
9	18
10	19
11	20
12	21
13	22
14	23

SATURDAY
18.09.2021

7
9
11
13
15
17
19
21
23

SUNDAY
19.09.2021

7
9
11
13
15
17
19
21
23

TO DO

- [ ] _____
- [ ] _____
- [ ] _____
- [ ] _____
- [ ] _____
- [ ] _____
- [ ] _____
- [ ] _____
- [ ] _____
- [ ] _____
- [ ] _____
- [ ] _____

- [ ] _____
- [ ] _____
- [ ] _____
- [ ] _____
- [ ] _____
- [ ] _____
- [ ] _____
- [ ] _____
- [ ] _____
- [ ] _____
- [ ] _____
- [ ] _____

NOTES

MONDAY
20.09.2021

6	15
7	16
8	17
9	18
10	19
11	20
12	21
13	22
14	23

TUESDAY
21.09.2021

6	15
7	16
8	17
9	18
10	19
11	20
12	21
13	22
14	23

WEDNESDAY
22.09.2021

6	15
7	16
8	17
9	18
10	19
11	20
12	21
13	22
14	23

TO DO

- [ ] _____
- [ ] _____
- [ ] _____
- [ ] _____
- [ ] _____
- [ ] _____
- [ ] _____
- [ ] _____
- [ ] _____
- [ ] _____
- [ ] _____
- [ ] _____

- [ ] _____
- [ ] _____
- [ ] _____
- [ ] _____
- [ ] _____
- [ ] _____
- [ ] _____
- [ ] _____
- [ ] _____
- [ ] _____
- [ ] _____
- [ ] _____

NOTES

THURSDAY
23.09.2021

6	15
7	16
8	17
9	18
10	19
11	20
12	21
13	22
14	23

FRIDAY
24.09.2021

6	15
7	16
8	17
9	18
10	19
11	20
12	21
13	22
14	23

SATURDAY
25.09.2021

7
9
11
13
15
17
19
21
23

SUNDAY
26.09.2021

7
9
11
13
15
17
19
21
23

TO DO

- [ ] _____
- [ ] _____
- [ ] _____
- [ ] _____
- [ ] _____
- [ ] _____
- [ ] _____
- [ ] _____
- [ ] _____
- [ ] _____
- [ ] _____
- [ ] _____

- [ ] _____
- [ ] _____
- [ ] _____
- [ ] _____
- [ ] _____
- [ ] _____
- [ ] _____
- [ ] _____
- [ ] _____
- [ ] _____
- [ ] _____
- [ ] _____

NOTES

_____

_____

_____

_____

_____

_____

_____

_____

_____

_____

_____

_____

MONDAY
27.09.2021

6	15
7	16
8	17
9	18
10	19
11	20
12	21
13	22
14	23

TUESDAY
28.09.2021

6	15
7	16
8	17
9	18
10	19
11	20
12	21
13	22
14	23

WEDNESDAY
29.09.2021

6	15
7	16
8	17
9	18
10	19
11	20
12	21
13	22
14	23

TO DO

- [ ] _____
- [ ] _____
- [ ] _____
- [ ] _____
- [ ] _____
- [ ] _____
- [ ] _____
- [ ] _____
- [ ] _____
- [ ] _____
- [ ] _____
- [ ] _____

- [ ] _____
- [ ] _____
- [ ] _____
- [ ] _____
- [ ] _____
- [ ] _____
- [ ] _____
- [ ] _____
- [ ] _____
- [ ] _____
- [ ] _____
- [ ] _____

NOTES

_____

_____

_____

_____

_____

_____

_____

_____

_____

_____

_____

_____

THURSDAY
30.09.2021

6	15
7	16
8	17
9	18
10	19
11	20
12	21
13	22
14	23

FRIDAY
01.10.2021

6	15
7	16
8	17
9	18
10	19
11	20
12	21
13	22
14	23

SATURDAY
02.10.2021

7	7
9	9
11	11
13	13
15	15
17	17
19	19
21	21
23	23

SUNDAY
03.10.2021

TO DO

- [ ] _____
- [ ] _____
- [ ] _____
- [ ] _____
- [ ] _____
- [ ] _____
- [ ] _____
- [ ] _____
- [ ] _____
- [ ] _____
- [ ] _____
- [ ] _____

- [ ] _____
- [ ] _____
- [ ] _____
- [ ] _____
- [ ] _____
- [ ] _____
- [ ] _____
- [ ] _____
- [ ] _____
- [ ] _____
- [ ] _____
- [ ] _____

NOTES

MONDAY
04.10.2021

6	15
7	16
8	17
9	18
10	19
11	20
12	21
13	22
14	23

TUESDAY
05.10.2021

6	15
7	16
8	17
9	18
10	19
11	20
12	21
13	22
14	23

WEDNESDAY
06.10.2021

6	15
7	16
8	17
9	18
10	19
11	20
12	21
13	22
14	23

TO DO

- [ ] _____
- [ ] _____
- [ ] _____
- [ ] _____
- [ ] _____
- [ ] _____
- [ ] _____
- [ ] _____
- [ ] _____
- [ ] _____
- [ ] _____

- [ ] _____
- [ ] _____
- [ ] _____
- [ ] _____
- [ ] _____
- [ ] _____
- [ ] _____
- [ ] _____
- [ ] _____
- [ ] _____
- [ ] _____

NOTES

_____

_____

_____

_____

_____

_____

_____

_____

_____

_____

_____

THURSDAY
07.10.2021

6	15
7	16
8	17
9	18
10	19
11	20
12	21
13	22
14	23

FRIDAY
08.10.2021

6	15
7	16
8	17
9	18
10	19
11	20
12	21
13	22
14	23

SATURDAY
09.10.2021

7
9
11
13
15
17
19
21
23

SUNDAY
10.10.2021

7
9
11
13
15
17
19
21
23

TO DO

- [ ] _____
- [ ] _____
- [ ] _____
- [ ] _____
- [ ] _____
- [ ] _____
- [ ] _____
- [ ] _____
- [ ] _____
- [ ] _____
- [ ] _____
- [ ] _____

- [ ] _____
- [ ] _____
- [ ] _____
- [ ] _____
- [ ] _____
- [ ] _____
- [ ] _____
- [ ] _____
- [ ] _____
- [ ] _____
- [ ] _____
- [ ] _____

NOTES

_____

_____

_____

_____

_____

_____

_____

_____

_____

_____

_____

MONDAY
11.10.2021

6	15
7	16
8	17
9	18
10	19
11	20
12	21
13	22
14	23

TUESDAY
12.10.2021

6	15
7	16
8	17
9	18
10	19
11	20
12	21
13	22
14	23

WEDNESDAY
13.10.2021

6	15
7	16
8	17
9	18
10	19
11	20
12	21
13	22
14	23

TO DO

- [ ] _____
- [ ] _____
- [ ] _____
- [ ] _____
- [ ] _____
- [ ] _____
- [ ] _____
- [ ] _____
- [ ] _____
- [ ] _____
- [ ] _____
- [ ] _____

- [ ] _____
- [ ] _____
- [ ] _____
- [ ] _____
- [ ] _____
- [ ] _____
- [ ] _____
- [ ] _____
- [ ] _____
- [ ] _____
- [ ] _____
- [ ] _____

NOTES

THURSDAY
14.10.2021

6	15
7	16
8	17
9	18
10	19
11	20
12	21
13	22
14	23

FRIDAY
15.10.2021

6	15
7	16
8	17
9	18
10	19
11	20
12	21
13	22
14	23

SATURDAY
16.10.2021

7
9
11
13
15
17
19
21
23

SUNDAY
17.10.2021

7
9
11
13
15
17
19
21
23

TO DO

- [ ] _____
- [ ] _____
- [ ] _____
- [ ] _____
- [ ] _____
- [ ] _____
- [ ] _____
- [ ] _____
- [ ] _____
- [ ] _____
- [ ] _____
- [ ] _____

- [ ] _____
- [ ] _____
- [ ] _____
- [ ] _____
- [ ] _____
- [ ] _____
- [ ] _____
- [ ] _____
- [ ] _____
- [ ] _____
- [ ] _____
- [ ] _____

NOTES

_____

_____

_____

_____

_____

_____

_____

_____

_____

_____

_____

_____

_____

MONDAY
18.10.2021

6	15
7	16
8	17
9	18
10	19
11	20
12	21
13	22
14	23

TUESDAY
19.10.2021

6	15
7	16
8	17
9	18
10	19
11	20
12	21
13	22
14	23

WEDNESDAY
20.10.2021

6	15
7	16
8	17
9	18
10	19
11	20
12	21
13	22
14	23

TO DO

- [ ]
- [ ]
- [ ]
- [ ]
- [ ]
- [ ]
- [ ]
- [ ]
- [ ]
- [ ]
- [ ]
- [ ]

- [ ]
- [ ]
- [ ]
- [ ]
- [ ]
- [ ]
- [ ]
- [ ]
- [ ]
- [ ]
- [ ]
- [ ]

NOTES

THURSDAY
21.10.2021

6	15
7	16
8	17
9	18
10	19
11	20
12	21
13	22
14	23

FRIDAY
22.10.2021

6	15
7	16
8	17
9	18
10	19
11	20
12	21
13	22
14	23

SATURDAY
23.10.2021

7
9
11
13
15
17
19
21
23

SUNDAY
24.10.2021

7
9
11
13
15
17
19
21
23

TO DO

- [ ] _____
- [ ] _____
- [ ] _____
- [ ] _____
- [ ] _____
- [ ] _____
- [ ] _____
- [ ] _____
- [ ] _____
- [ ] _____
- [ ] _____
- [ ] _____

- [ ] _____
- [ ] _____
- [ ] _____
- [ ] _____
- [ ] _____
- [ ] _____
- [ ] _____
- [ ] _____
- [ ] _____
- [ ] _____
- [ ] _____
- [ ] _____

NOTES

_____

_____

_____

_____

_____

_____

_____

_____

_____

_____

_____

_____

MONDAY
25.10.2021

6	15
7	16
8	17
9	18
10	19
11	20
12	21
13	22
14	23

TUESDAY
26.10.2021

6	15
7	16
8	17
9	18
10	19
11	20
12	21
13	22
14	23

WEDNESDAY
27.10.2021

6	15
7	16
8	17
9	18
10	19
11	20
12	21
13	22
14	23

TO DO

- [ ] _____
- [ ] _____
- [ ] _____
- [ ] _____
- [ ] _____
- [ ] _____
- [ ] _____
- [ ] _____
- [ ] _____
- [ ] _____
- [ ] _____
- [ ] _____

- [ ] _____
- [ ] _____
- [ ] _____
- [ ] _____
- [ ] _____
- [ ] _____
- [ ] _____
- [ ] _____
- [ ] _____
- [ ] _____
- [ ] _____
- [ ] _____

NOTES

THURSDAY
28.10.2021

6	15
7	16
8	17
9	18
10	19
11	20
12	21
13	22
14	23

FRIDAY
29.10.2021

6	15
7	16
8	17
9	18
10	19
11	20
12	21
13	22
14	23

SATURDAY
30.10.2021

7
9
11
13
15
17
19
21
23

SUNDAY
31.10.2021

7
9
11
13
15
17
19
21
23

TO DO

- [ ] _____
- [ ] _____
- [ ] _____
- [ ] _____
- [ ] _____
- [ ] _____
- [ ] _____
- [ ] _____
- [ ] _____
- [ ] _____
- [ ] _____
- [ ] _____

- [ ] _____
- [ ] _____
- [ ] _____
- [ ] _____
- [ ] _____
- [ ] _____
- [ ] _____
- [ ] _____
- [ ] _____
- [ ] _____
- [ ] _____
- [ ] _____

NOTES

_____

_____

_____

_____

_____

_____

_____

_____

_____

_____

_____

_____

MONDAY
01.11.2021

6	15
7	16
8	17
9	18
10	19
11	20
12	21
13	22
14	23

TUESDAY
02.11.2021

6	15
7	16
8	17
9	18
10	19
11	20
12	21
13	22
14	23

WEDNESDAY
03.11.2021

6	15
7	16
8	17
9	18
10	19
11	20
12	21
13	22
14	23

TO DO

☐ _____   ☐ _____
☐ _____   ☐ _____
☐ _____   ☐ _____
☐ _____   ☐ _____
☐ _____   ☐ _____
☐ _____   ☐ _____
☐ _____   ☐ _____
☐ _____   ☐ _____
☐ _____   ☐ _____
☐ _____   ☐ _____
☐ _____   ☐ _____
☐ _____   ☐ _____

NOTES

_____
_____
_____
_____
_____
_____
_____
_____
_____
_____
_____
_____
_____

THURSDAY
04.11.2021

6	15
7	16
8	17
9	18
10	19
11	20
12	21
13	22
14	23

FRIDAY
05.11.2021

6	15
7	16
8	17
9	18
10	19
11	20
12	21
13	22
14	23

SATURDAY
06.11.2021

7	
9	
11	
13	
15	
17	
19	
21	
23	

SUNDAY
07.11.2021

7	
9	
11	
13	
15	
17	
19	
21	
23	

TO DO

☐ _____   ☐ _____
☐ _____   ☐ _____
☐ _____   ☐ _____
☐ _____   ☐ _____
☐ _____   ☐ _____
☐ _____   ☐ _____
☐ _____   ☐ _____
☐ _____   ☐ _____
☐ _____   ☐ _____
☐ _____   ☐ _____
☐ _____   ☐ _____
☐ _____   ☐ _____

NOTES

_____
_____
_____
_____
_____
_____
_____
_____
_____
_____
_____
_____

MONDAY
08.11.2021

6	15
7	16
8	17
9	18
10	19
11	20
12	21
13	22
14	23

TUESDAY
09.11.2021

6	15
7	16
8	17
9	18
10	19
11	20
12	21
13	22
14	23

WEDNESDAY
10.11.2021

6	15
7	16
8	17
9	18
10	19
11	20
12	21
13	22
14	23

TO DO

- [ ] _____
- [ ] _____
- [ ] _____
- [ ] _____
- [ ] _____
- [ ] _____
- [ ] _____
- [ ] _____
- [ ] _____
- [ ] _____
- [ ] _____
- [ ] _____

- [ ] _____
- [ ] _____
- [ ] _____
- [ ] _____
- [ ] _____
- [ ] _____
- [ ] _____
- [ ] _____
- [ ] _____
- [ ] _____
- [ ] _____
- [ ] _____

NOTES

THURSDAY
11.11.2021

6	15
7	16
8	17
9	18
10	19
11	20
12	21
13	22
14	23

FRIDAY
12.11.2021

6	15
7	16
8	17
9	18
10	19
11	20
12	21
13	22
14	23

SATURDAY
13.11.2021

7
9
11
13
15
17
19
21
23

SUNDAY
14.11.2021

7
9
11
13
15
17
19
21
23

TO DO

- [ ]
- [ ]
- [ ]
- [ ]
- [ ]
- [ ]
- [ ]
- [ ]
- [ ]
- [ ]
- [ ]
- [ ]
- [ ]
- [ ]
- [ ]
- [ ]
- [ ]
- [ ]
- [ ]
- [ ]
- [ ]
- [ ]
- [ ]
- [ ]

NOTES

MONDAY
15.11.2021

6	15
7	16
8	17
9	18
10	19
11	20
12	21
13	22
14	23

TUESDAY
16.11.2021

6	15
7	16
8	17
9	18
10	19
11	20
12	21
13	22
14	23

WEDNESDAY
17.11.2021

6	15
7	16
8	17
9	18
10	19
11	20
12	21
13	22
14	23

TO DO

- [ ] _____
- [ ] _____
- [ ] _____
- [ ] _____
- [ ] _____
- [ ] _____
- [ ] _____
- [ ] _____
- [ ] _____
- [ ] _____
- [ ] _____
- [ ] _____

- [ ] _____
- [ ] _____
- [ ] _____
- [ ] _____
- [ ] _____
- [ ] _____
- [ ] _____
- [ ] _____
- [ ] _____
- [ ] _____
- [ ] _____
- [ ] _____

NOTES

_____

_____

_____

_____

_____

_____

_____

_____

_____

_____

_____

_____

_____

THURSDAY
18.11.2021

6	15
7	16
8	17
9	18
10	19
11	20
12	21
13	22
14	23

FRIDAY
19.11.2021

6	15
7	16
8	17
9	18
10	19
11	20
12	21
13	22
14	23

SATURDAY
20.11.2021

7
9
11
13
15
17
19
21
23

SUNDAY
21.11.2021

7
9
11
13
15
17
19
21
23

TO DO

- [ ] _____
- [ ] _____
- [ ] _____
- [ ] _____
- [ ] _____
- [ ] _____
- [ ] _____
- [ ] _____
- [ ] _____
- [ ] _____
- [ ] _____
- [ ] _____

- [ ] _____
- [ ] _____
- [ ] _____
- [ ] _____
- [ ] _____
- [ ] _____
- [ ] _____
- [ ] _____
- [ ] _____
- [ ] _____
- [ ] _____
- [ ] _____

NOTES

_____

_____

_____

_____

_____

_____

_____

_____

_____

_____

_____

_____

_____

MONDAY
22.11.2021

6	15
7	16
8	17
9	18
10	19
11	20
12	21
13	22
14	23

TUESDAY
23.11.2021

6	15
7	16
8	17
9	18
10	19
11	20
12	21
13	22
14	23

WEDNESDAY
24.11.2021

6	15
7	16
8	17
9	18
10	19
11	20
12	21
13	22
14	23

TO DO

- [ ]
- [ ]
- [ ]
- [ ]
- [ ]
- [ ]
- [ ]
- [ ]
- [ ]
- [ ]
- [ ]
- [ ]

- [ ]
- [ ]
- [ ]
- [ ]
- [ ]
- [ ]
- [ ]
- [ ]
- [ ]
- [ ]
- [ ]
- [ ]

NOTES

THURSDAY
25.11.2021

6		15	
7		16	
8		17	
9		18	
10		19	
11		20	
12		21	
13		22	
14		23	

FRIDAY
26.11.2021

6		15	
7		16	
8		17	
9		18	
10		19	
11		20	
12		21	
13		22	
14		23	

SATURDAY
27.11.2021

7	
9	
11	
13	
15	
17	
19	
21	
23	

SUNDAY
28.11.2021

7	
9	
11	
13	
15	
17	
19	
21	
23	

TO DO

☐ _____ ☐ _____
☐ _____ ☐ _____
☐ _____ ☐ _____
☐ _____ ☐ _____
☐ _____ ☐ _____
☐ _____ ☐ _____
☐ _____ ☐ _____
☐ _____ ☐ _____
☐ _____ ☐ _____
☐ _____ ☐ _____
☐ _____ ☐ _____
☐ _____ ☐ _____

NOTES

_____
_____
_____
_____
_____
_____
_____
_____
_____
_____
_____

MONDAY
29.11.2021

6	15
7	16
8	17
9	18
10	19
11	20
12	21
13	22
14	23

TUESDAY
30.11.2021

6	15
7	16
8	17
9	18
10	19
11	20
12	21
13	22
14	23

WEDNESDAY
01.12.2021

6	15
7	16
8	17
9	18
10	19
11	20
12	21
13	22
14	23

TO DO

- [ ] _____
- [ ] _____
- [ ] _____
- [ ] _____
- [ ] _____
- [ ] _____
- [ ] _____
- [ ] _____
- [ ] _____
- [ ] _____
- [ ] _____
- [ ] _____

- [ ] _____
- [ ] _____
- [ ] _____
- [ ] _____
- [ ] _____
- [ ] _____
- [ ] _____
- [ ] _____
- [ ] _____
- [ ] _____
- [ ] _____
- [ ] _____

NOTES

THURSDAY
02.12.2021

6	15
7	16
8	17
9	18
10	19
11	20
12	21
13	22
14	23

FRIDAY
03.12.2021

6	15
7	16
8	17
9	18
10	19
11	20
12	21
13	22
14	23

SATURDAY
04.12.2021

7	9
11	13
15	17
19	21
23	

SUNDAY
05.12.2021

7	9
11	13
15	17
19	21
23	

TO DO

- [ ] _____
- [ ] _____
- [ ] _____
- [ ] _____
- [ ] _____
- [ ] _____
- [ ] _____
- [ ] _____
- [ ] _____
- [ ] _____
- [ ] _____
- [ ] _____

- [ ] _____
- [ ] _____
- [ ] _____
- [ ] _____
- [ ] _____
- [ ] _____
- [ ] _____
- [ ] _____
- [ ] _____
- [ ] _____
- [ ] _____
- [ ] _____

NOTES

_____
_____
_____
_____
_____
_____
_____
_____
_____
_____
_____
_____
_____

MONDAY
06.12.2021

6	15
7	16
8	17
9	18
10	19
11	20
12	21
13	22
14	23

TUESDAY
07.12.2021

6	15
7	16
8	17
9	18
10	19
11	20
12	21
13	22
14	23

WEDNESDAY
08.12.2021

6	15
7	16
8	17
9	18
10	19
11	20
12	21
13	22
14	23

TO DO

- [ ] _____
- [ ] _____
- [ ] _____
- [ ] _____
- [ ] _____
- [ ] _____
- [ ] _____
- [ ] _____
- [ ] _____
- [ ] _____
- [ ] _____
- [ ] _____

- [ ] _____
- [ ] _____
- [ ] _____
- [ ] _____
- [ ] _____
- [ ] _____
- [ ] _____
- [ ] _____
- [ ] _____
- [ ] _____
- [ ] _____
- [ ] _____

NOTES

_____
_____
_____
_____
_____
_____
_____
_____
_____
_____
_____
_____
_____

THURSDAY
09.12.2021

6		15	
7		16	
8		17	
9		18	
10		19	
11		20	
12		21	
13		22	
14		23	

FRIDAY
10.12.2021

6		15	
7		16	
8		17	
9		18	
10		19	
11		20	
12		21	
13		22	
14		23	

SATURDAY
11.12.2021

7	
9	
11	
13	
15	
17	
19	
21	
23	

SUNDAY
12.12.2021

7	
9	
11	
13	
15	
17	
19	
21	
23	

TO DO

☐ _____   ☐ _____
☐ _____   ☐ _____
☐ _____   ☐ _____
☐ _____   ☐ _____
☐ _____   ☐ _____
☐ _____   ☐ _____
☐ _____   ☐ _____
☐ _____   ☐ _____
☐ _____   ☐ _____
☐ _____   ☐ _____
☐ _____   ☐ _____
☐ _____   ☐ _____

NOTES

_____
_____
_____
_____
_____
_____
_____
_____
_____
_____
_____
_____
_____

MONDAY
13.12.2021

6	15
7	16
8	17
9	18
10	19
11	20
12	21
13	22
14	23

TUESDAY
14.12.2021

6	15
7	16
8	17
9	18
10	19
11	20
12	21
13	22
14	23

WEDNESDAY
15.12.2021

6	15
7	16
8	17
9	18
10	19
11	20
12	21
13	22
14	23

TO DO

- [ ] _____
- [ ] _____
- [ ] _____
- [ ] _____
- [ ] _____
- [ ] _____
- [ ] _____
- [ ] _____
- [ ] _____
- [ ] _____
- [ ] _____
- [ ] _____

- [ ] _____
- [ ] _____
- [ ] _____
- [ ] _____
- [ ] _____
- [ ] _____
- [ ] _____
- [ ] _____
- [ ] _____
- [ ] _____
- [ ] _____
- [ ] _____

NOTES

_____

_____

_____

_____

_____

_____

_____

_____

_____

_____

_____

_____

THURSDAY
16.12.2021

6	15
7	16
8	17
9	18
10	19
11	20
12	21
13	22
14	23

FRIDAY
17.12.2021

6	15
7	16
8	17
9	18
10	19
11	20
12	21
13	22
14	23

SATURDAY
18.12.2021

7
9
11
13
15
17
19
21
23

SUNDAY
19.12.2021

7
9
11
13
15
17
19
21
23

TO DO

- [ ] _____
- [ ] _____
- [ ] _____
- [ ] _____
- [ ] _____
- [ ] _____
- [ ] _____
- [ ] _____
- [ ] _____
- [ ] _____
- [ ] _____
- [ ] _____

- [ ] _____
- [ ] _____
- [ ] _____
- [ ] _____
- [ ] _____
- [ ] _____
- [ ] _____
- [ ] _____
- [ ] _____
- [ ] _____
- [ ] _____
- [ ] _____

NOTES

_____

_____

_____

_____

_____

_____

_____

_____

_____

_____

_____

_____

_____

MONDAY
20.12.2021

6	15
7	16
8	17
9	18
10	19
11	20
12	21
13	22
14	23

TUESDAY
21.12.2021

6	15
7	16
8	17
9	18
10	19
11	20
12	21
13	22
14	23

WEDNESDAY
22.12.2021

6	15
7	16
8	17
9	18
10	19
11	20
12	21
13	22
14	23

TO DO

- [ ] _____
- [ ] _____
- [ ] _____
- [ ] _____
- [ ] _____
- [ ] _____
- [ ] _____
- [ ] _____
- [ ] _____
- [ ] _____
- [ ] _____
- [ ] _____

- [ ] _____
- [ ] _____
- [ ] _____
- [ ] _____
- [ ] _____
- [ ] _____
- [ ] _____
- [ ] _____
- [ ] _____
- [ ] _____
- [ ] _____
- [ ] _____

NOTES

_____

_____

_____

_____

_____

_____

_____

_____

_____

_____

_____

_____

THURSDAY
23.12.2021

6	15
7	16
8	17
9	18
10	19
11	20
12	21
13	22
14	23

FRIDAY
24.12.2021

6	15
7	16
8	17
9	18
10	19
11	20
12	21
13	22
14	23

SATURDAY
25.12.2021

7	
9	
11	
13	
15	
17	
19	
21	
23	

SUNDAY
26.12.2021

7	
9	
11	
13	
15	
17	
19	
21	
23	

TO DO

- [ ]
- [ ]
- [ ]
- [ ]
- [ ]
- [ ]
- [ ]
- [ ]
- [ ]
- [ ]
- [ ]
- [ ]

- [ ]
- [ ]
- [ ]
- [ ]
- [ ]
- [ ]
- [ ]
- [ ]
- [ ]
- [ ]
- [ ]
- [ ]

NOTES

MONDAY
27.12.2021

6	15
7	16
8	17
9	18
10	19
11	20
12	21
13	22
14	23

TUESDAY
28.12.2021

6	15
7	16
8	17
9	18
10	19
11	20
12	21
13	22
14	23

WEDNESDAY
29.12.2021

6	15
7	16
8	17
9	18
10	19
11	20
12	21
13	22
14	23

TO DO

- [ ] _____
- [ ] _____
- [ ] _____
- [ ] _____
- [ ] _____
- [ ] _____
- [ ] _____
- [ ] _____
- [ ] _____
- [ ] _____
- [ ] _____
- [ ] _____

- [ ] _____
- [ ] _____
- [ ] _____
- [ ] _____
- [ ] _____
- [ ] _____
- [ ] _____
- [ ] _____
- [ ] _____
- [ ] _____
- [ ] _____
- [ ] _____

NOTES

THURSDAY
30.12.2021

6	15
7	16
8	17
9	18
10	19
11	20
12	21
13	22
14	23

FRIDAY
31.12.2021

6	15
7	16
8	17
9	18
10	19
11	20
12	21
13	22
14	23

SATURDAY
01.01.2022

7
9
11
13
15
17
19
21
23

SUNDAY
02.01.2022

7
9
11
13
15
17
19
21
23

TO DO

- [ ] _____
- [ ] _____
- [ ] _____
- [ ] _____
- [ ] _____
- [ ] _____
- [ ] _____
- [ ] _____
- [ ] _____
- [ ] _____
- [ ] _____
- [ ] _____

- [ ] _____
- [ ] _____
- [ ] _____
- [ ] _____
- [ ] _____
- [ ] _____
- [ ] _____
- [ ] _____
- [ ] _____
- [ ] _____
- [ ] _____
- [ ] _____

NOTES

_____

_____

_____

_____

_____

_____

_____

_____

_____

_____

_____

_____

_____

NOTES

NOTES

NOTES

NOTES

2021

JANUARY

Mo	Tue	Wed	Thu	Fri	Sat	Sun
28	29	30	31	1	2	3
4	5	6	7	8	9	10
11	12	13	14	15	16	17
18	19	20	21	22	23	24
25	26	27	28	29	30	31

FEBRUARY

Mo	Tue	Wed	Thu	Fri	Sat	Sun
1	2	3	4	5	6	7
8	9	10	11	12	13	14
15	16	17	18	19	20	21
22	23	24	25	26	27	28
1	2	3	4	5	6	7

MARCH

Mo	Tue	Wed	Thu	Fri	Sat	Sun
1	2	3	4	5	6	7
8	9	10	11	12	13	14
15	16	17	18	19	20	21
22	23	24	25	26	27	28
29	30	31	1	2	3	4

APRIL

Mo	Tue	Wed	Thu	Fri	Sat	Sun
29	30	31	1	2	3	4
5	6	7	8	9	10	11
12	13	14	15	16	17	18
19	20	21	22	23	24	25
26	27	28	29	30	1	2

MAY

Mo	Tue	Wed	Thu	Fri	Sat	Sun
26	27	28	29	30	1	2
3	4	5	6	7	8	9
10	11	12	13	14	15	16
17	18	19	20	21	22	23
24	25	26	27	28	29	30
31	1	2	3	4	5	6

JUNE

Mo	Tue	Wed	Thu	Fri	Sat	Sun
31	1	2	3	4	5	6
7	8	9	10	11	12	13
14	15	16	17	18	19	20
21	22	23	24	25	26	27
28	29	30	1	2	3	4

2 0 2 1

JULY

Mo	Tue	Wed	Thu	Fri	Sat	Sun
28	29	30	1	2	3	4
5	6	7	8	9	10	11
12	13	14	15	16	17	18
19	20	21	22	23	24	25
26	27	28	29	30	31	1

AUGUST

Mo	Tue	Wed	Thu	Fri	Sat	Sun
26	27	28	29	30	31	1
2	3	4	5	6	7	8
9	10	11	12	13	14	15
16	17	18	19	20	21	22
23	24	25	26	27	28	29
30	31	1	2	3	4	5

SEPTEMBER

Mo	Tue	Wed	Thu	Fri	Sat	Sun
30	31	1	2	3	4	5
6	7	8	9	10	11	12
13	14	15	16	17	18	19
20	21	22	23	24	25	26
27	28	29	30	1	2	3

OCTOBER

Mo	Tue	Wed	Thu	Fri	Sat	Sun
27	28	29	30	1	2	3
4	5	6	7	8	9	10
11	12	13	14	15	16	17
18	19	20	21	22	23	24
25	26	27	28	29	30	31

NOVEMBER

Mo	Tue	Wed	Thu	Fri	Sat	Sun
1	2	3	4	5	6	7
8	9	10	11	12	13	14
15	16	17	18	19	20	21
22	23	24	25	26	27	28
29	30	1	2	3	4	5

DECEMBER

Mo	Tue	Wed	Thu	Fri	Sat	Sun
29	30	1	2	3	4	5
6	7	8	9	10	11	12
13	14	15	16	17	18	19
20	21	22	23	24	25	26
27	28	29	30	31	1	2

WORKOUT SCHEDULE

DAY	MONDAY	TUESDAY	WEDNESDAY	THURSDAY	FRIDAY	SATURDAY	SUNDAY
FOCUS							
TIME							

SUCCESS TRACKER

	JAN	FEB	MAR	APR	MAY	JUN	JUL	AUG	SEP	OCT	NOV	DEC
1												
2												
3												
4												
5												
6												
7												
8												
9												
10												
11												
12												
13												
14												
15												
16												
17												
18												
19												
20												
21												
22												
23												
24												
25												
26												
27												
28												
29												
30												
31												

HOUSEHOLD SCHEDULE

TASK	WEEKDAY	FREQUENCY

BUDGET TRACKER

MONTH	INCOME	OUTGOINGS	DIFFERENCE
JANUARY	+	-	=
FEBRUARY	+	-	=
MARCH	+	-	=
APRIL	+	-	=
MAY	+	-	=
JUNE	+	-	=
JULY	+	-	=
AUGUST	+	-	=
SEPTEMBER	+	-	=
OCTOBER	+	-	=
NOVEMBER	+	-	=
DECEMBER	+	-	=

CONTACT

Website:
www.linamariew.com
www.linawalbracht.de

Instagram:
@linamariew
@linawalbracht

E-Mail:
simply@linamariew.com